Georgia

The Peach State

Karen Diane Haywood, Jessica Cohn, and Laura L. Sullivan

Cavendish
Square

New York

Published in 2016 by Cavendish Square Publishing, LLC
243 5th Avenue, Suite 136, New York, NY 10016

Library of Congress Cataloging-in-Publication Data

Sullivan, Laura L., 1974-
Georgia / Laura L. Sullivan, Karen Diane Haywood, and Jessica Cohn.
pages cm
Includes bibliographical references and index.
ISBN 978-1-62713-192-6 (hardcover) ISBN 978-1-62713-194-0 (ebook)
1. Georgia—Juvenile literature. I. Haywood, Karen Diane. II. Cohn, Jessica. III. Title.

F286.3.S86 2016
975.8—dc23

2014049272

Editorial Director: David McNamara
Editor: Fletcher Doyle
Copy Editor: Rebecca Rohan
Art Director: Jeffrey Talbot
Designer: Stephanie Flecha
Senior Production Manager: Jennifer Ryder-Talbot
Production Editor: Renni Johnson
Photo Research by J8 Media

The photographs in this book are used by permission and through the courtesy of: Tetra Images/Brand X Pictures/Getty Images, cover; Fred Whitehead/Superstock, 4; Daniel Prudek/Shutterstock.com, 4; Lee Canfield/Superstock, 4; Animals Animals/Superstock, 5; NHPA/Superstock, 5; Darryl Brooks/Shutterstock.com, 5; Rolf_52/Shutterstock.com, 6; Westgraphix LLC, 8; Ken Martin/Alamy, 11; Mark Newman/Superstock, 13; AP Photo/stf, 14; Buddy Mays/Alamy, 14; f11photo/Shutterstock.com, 14; Brian Lasenby/Shutterstock.com, 15; Ffooter/Shutterstock.com, 15; Michael Adams/File:Apatosaurus at Tellus.JPG/Wikimedia Commons, 15; Corbis Nomad/Alamy, 16; Craig Loose/Alamy, 18; Danita Delimont/Alamy, 20; imagebrokers.net/Superstock, 20; Animals Animals/Superstock, 20; Debbie Steinhausser/Shutterstock.com, 21; Patrick K. Campbell/Shutterstock.com, 21; AwakenedEye/iStock/Thinkstock, 21; Richard Ellis / Alamy, 22; Tami Chappell/Getty Images, 24; North Wind Picture Archives/Alamy, 25; Marilyn Angel Wynn/Getty Images, 26; A. I. Keller/File:Siege of Savannah A.I. Keller.jpg/Wikimedia Commons, 28; Superstock, 29; Mark Gail/The Washington Post/Getty Images, 30; North Wind Picture Archives/Alamy, 31; Buyenlarge/Getty Images, 32; John Van Hasselt/Corbis, 33; Danny E Hooks/Shutterstock.com, 34; Sean Pavone/Shutterstock.com, 34; Glenn Grossman/File:Chblossomfest.JPG/Wikimedia Commons, 35; Michael Rivera/File:Eighth note and a treble clef, Ray Charles Plaza.JPG/Wikimedia Commons, 35; Library of Congress, 36; AP Photo/CFW, 38; Time & Life Pictures/Getty Images, 40; Bill Cobb/Superstock, 41; Blulz60/Shutterstock.com, 44; Kevin Fleming/Corbis, 46; AP Photo/JNK, 47; Culver Pictures, Inc./Superstock, 48; S_Bukley/Shutterstock.com, 48; Underwood and Underwood, New York/File:Juliette Gordon Low 1923.jpg/Wikimedia Commons, 48; Everett Collection/Superstock, 49; Everett Collection, Inc./Alamy, 49; Everett Collection/Shutterstock.com, 49; Accurate Art, 50; Robert Marmion/Alamy, 51; AP Photo/Charles Dharapak, 53; JTB Photo Communications, Inc./Alamy, 54; Paras Griffin/Getty Images, 54; Sharmin Ayoub/NPS, 55; AP Photo/Stephen Morton/Corbis, 55; AP Photo/Atlanta Journal & Constitution, Jason Getz, 56; Superstock, 58; AP Photo/David Goldman, 60; Exactostock/Superstock, 61; Allstar Picture Library/Alamy, 62; Davis Turner/Getty Images, 62; Rick Friedman/CNP/Getty Images, 62; AP Photo/Atlanta JournalConstitution,Jason Getz, 63; f11photo / Shutterstock.com, 64; Michael Rutherford/Superstock, 66; Scott Barrow, Inc./Superstock, 67; AP Photo/Lockheed Martin, John Rossino, 68; David R. Frazier Photolibrary, Inc./Alamy, 68; Paul Giamou/Getty Images, 69; Jeff Greenberg/Alamy, 69; StephanieFrey/iStock/Thinkstock, 70; PRNewsFoto/Kia Motors Corporation, Erik S. Lesser, 71; Visions of America/Superstock, 73; Christopher Santoro, 74; /khoroshkov/iStock/Thinkstock, 75; Kelly vanDellen/Shutterstock.com, 75; Christopher Santoro, 76; Christopher Santoro, 76.

Printed in the United States of America

GEORGIA

CONTENTS

State Tree: Live Oak

The live oak became the state tree in 1937. In Georgia, live oaks grow inland, along the coastal plain, and on the barrier islands. The largest live oak in the state is nicknamed the Village Sentinel. It is in Waycross, and stands 86 feet (26 meters) high.

State Insect: Honeybee

Honeybees make a valuable contribution to Georgia's economy. In addition to producing honey, they cross-pollinate many crops. By naming the honeybee the state insect in 1975, officials recognized its importance to the state's agricultural interests.

State Bird: Brown Thrasher

The brown thrasher inspired the name of Georgia's former National Hockey League team. The thrasher is about 1 foot (0.3 m) long. Its tail makes up nearly half its length. The thrasher feeds mainly on insects. The thrasher tosses aside leaves with its beak while searching for food on the ground.

★ State Fish: Largemouth Bass

In 1970, Georgia's legislature made this popular game fish the official state fish. It is the largest of black basses. Largemouth bass can weigh more than 12 pounds (5 kilograms) and grow longer than 25 inches (64 centimeters).

★ State Reptile: Gopher Tortoise

Designated the state reptile in 1989, the gopher tortoise is one of the oldest living species **native** to the state. This special land tortoise is now listed as threatened—at risk of becoming endangered. It is illegal to keep one as a pet. In the wild, the gopher tortoise digs burrows up to 40 feet (12 m) long and 10 feet (3 m) deep.

★ State Prepared Food: Grits

Grits became Georgia's official prepared food in 2002. Made of ground corn, grits are a traditional Southern food. Many people add meat, vegetables, fruit, seasonings, or sweeteners to this popular dish.

The Mercer House is one of the most well-known mansions in Savannah.

The Peach State

Georgia's landscape offers a variety of geographic features, from the high peaks and deep valleys of the Appalachian Mountains in the north to the southern swamps and plains. The Peach State is divided into 159 counties and several distinctive land regions. In addition to its two most famous cities—historic Savannah and modern Atlanta—Georgia boasts stately **plantation** homes, historic small towns, the world's largest azalea garden, and the mysterious and wild Okefenokee Swamp.

Georgia is the largest state east of the Mississippi River, in terms of land area. It covers 57,513 square miles (148,958 sq km). Mountains rim the north, coastal plains cover the south, and the central part of the state features rolling hills. The state has six main land regions. The Gulf Coastal Plain covers the southwest region, and the Atlantic Coastal Plain is in the southeast, reaching eastward to the Atlantic Ocean. The Blue Ridge Mountains (part of the Appalachians) are situated in the northeast. The Appalachian Plateau and the Appalachian Ridge and Valley region mark the northwestern corner. The Piedmont Plateau sweeps across the middle of the state.

GEORGIA
COUNTY MAP

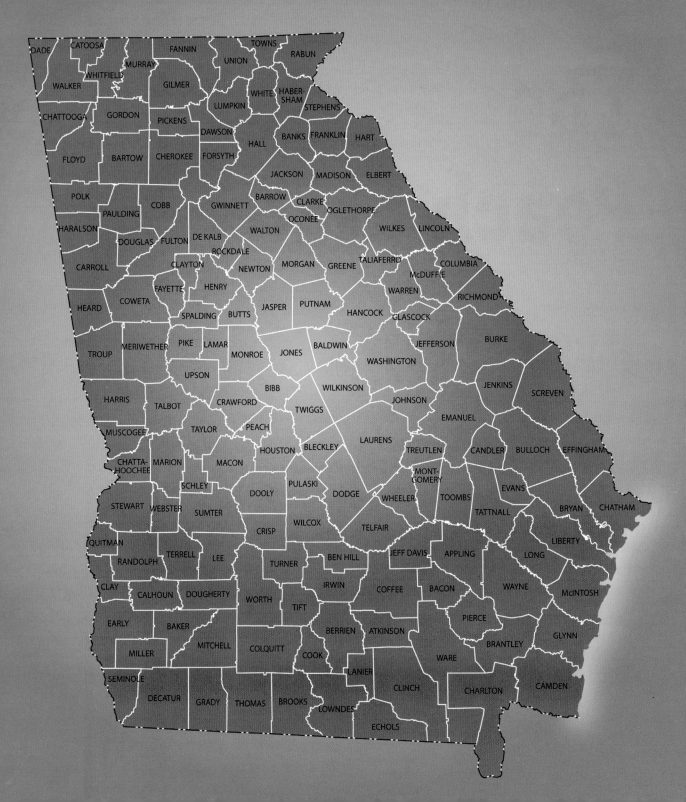

GEORGIA

POPULATION BY COUNTY

County	Population	County	Population	County	Population	County	Population
Appling	18,368	Cherokee	221,315	Fannin	23,492		
Atkinson	8,284	Clarke	120,266	Fayette	107,524		
Bacon	11,198	Clay	3,116	Floyd	96,177		
Baker	3,366	Clayton	265,888	Forsyth	187,928		
Baldwin	46,367	Clinch	6,718	Franklin	21,894		
Banks	18,316	Cobb	707,442	Fulton	977,773		
Barrow	70,169	Coffee	43,170	Gilmer	28,190		
Bartow	100,661	Colquitt	46,137	Glascock	3,142		
Ben Hill	17,538	Columbia	131,627	Glynn	81,022		
Berrien	19,041	Cook	16,923	Gordon	55,766		
Bibb	156,462	Coweta	130,929	Grady	25,440		
Bleckley	12,913	Crawford	12,600	Greene	16,092		
Brantley	18,587	Crisp	23,606	Gwinnett	842,046		
Brooks	15,403	Dade	16,490	Habersham	43,520		
Bryan	32,214	Dawson	22,422	Hall	185,416		
Bulloch	72,694	Decatur	27,509	Hancock	8,996		
Burke	23,125	De Kalb	707,089	Haralson	28,400		
Butts	23,524	Dodge	21,329	Harris	32,550		
Calhoun	6,504	Dooly	14,318	Hart	25,518		
Camden	51,402	Dougherty	94,501	Heard	11,633		
Candler	11,117	Douglas	133,971	Henry	209,053		
Carroll	111,580	Early	10,594	Houston	146,136		
Catoosa	65,046	Echols	3,988	Irwin	9,600		
Charlton	13,295	Effingham	53,293	Jackson	60,571		
Chatham	276,434	Elbert	19,684	Jasper	13,630		
Chattahoochee	13,037	Emanuel	22,898	Jeff Davis	15,156		
Chattooga	25,725	Evans	10,689	Jefferson	16,432		

GEORGIA

POPULATION BY COUNTY

County	Population	County	Population	County	Population
Jenkins	9,213	Oglethorpe	14,618	Thomas	44,724
Johnson	9,897	Paulding	144,800	Tift	41,064
Jones	28,577	Peach	27,622	Toombs	27,315
Lamar	18,057	Pickens	29,268	Towns	10,495
Lanier	10,400	Pierce	18,844	Treutlen	6,769
Laurens	48,041	Pike	17,810	Troup	68,468
Lee	28,746	Polk	41,188	Turner	8,410
Liberty	65,471	Pulaski	11,720	Twiggs	8,447
Lincoln	7,737	Putnam	21,198	Union	21,451
Long	16,048	Quitman	2,404	Upson	26,630
Lowndes	114,552	Rabun	16,297	Walker	68,094
Lumpkin	30,611	Randolph	7,327	Walton	84,575
Macon	14,263	Richmond	202,587	Ware	35,821
Madison	27,922	Rockdale	85,820	Warren	5,578
Marion	8,711	Schley	4,990	Washington	20,879
McDuffie	21,663	Screven	14,202	Wayne	30,305
McIntosh	13,839	Seminole	8,947	Webster	2,793
Meriwether	21,273	Spalding	63,865	Wheeler	7,888
Miller	5,969	Stephens	25,891	White	27,556
Mitchell	23,144	Stewart	6,042	Whitfield	103,359
Monroe	26,637	Sumter	31,554	Wilcox	9,068
Montgomery	8,913	Talbot	6,517	Wilkes	10,076
Morgan	17,881	Taliaferro	1,680	Wilkinson	9,577
Murray	39,392	Tattnall	25,384	Worth	21,741
Muscogee	198,413	Taylor	8,420		
Newton	101,505	Telfair	16,349		
Oconee	33,619	Terrell	9,045		

Source: US Bureau of the Census, 2010

The Cohutta Wilderness, which covers 40,000 acres (16,000 hectares), is shared by Georgia and Tennessee.

The Northern Landscape

In northeastern Georgia, the Blue Ridge Mountains rise out of the broad valleys and forest-covered ridges of the foothills. Millions of people have explored this region by walking along the Appalachian National Scenic Trail. This famous footpath starts in Georgia at Springer Mountain and curves northward past Blood and Big Cedar Mountains. It reaches north more than 2,000 miles (3,200 km) to Mount Katahdin in Maine.

The northwestern corner is part of the Appalachian Plateau, which extends from New York south to Georgia and Alabama. A plateau is a flat-topped portion of land that sits above the surrounding region. The plateau in Georgia was lifted upward during the time the Appalachians formed. Just south of this rugged surface is the Appalachian Ridge and Valley region, a belt of scenic mountains known for their even ridges and long valleys.

Georgia Borders

North: North Carolina
Tennessee

South: Florida

East: South Carolina
Atlantic Ocean

West: Alabama

The Cohutta Wilderness, which Georgia shares with Tennessee, can also be found in the northwestern part of the state. Here, mountains house caves and canyons that have—so far—been largely unaffected by tourism and development.

The Piedmont

The state capital, Atlanta, is located on the Piedmont Plateau. This central region is characterized by gently rolling hills and the red clay soil that Georgia is famous for. Atlanta is about 50 miles (80 km) south of the Appalachians. However, the Atlanta area ranges in elevation from about 850 feet to 1,100 feet (260 m to 340 m) and has several mountains that rise 300 feet to 800 feet (90 m to 240 m) higher. Just east of Atlanta is Stone Mountain, a monstrous mound of gray rock 825 feet (251 m) tall.

At the western end of the Piedmont Plateau, Pine Mountain rises from the plains near Warm Springs. At 1,500 feet (460 m) in elevation, Pine Mountain is a popular area for Georgians to find relief from the summer heat and to soak in the hot mineral springs that bubble up from the mountainside.

The South

While the famous Georgia peach is grown mainly in the valleys of the Piedmont, the south is where peanuts, pecans, and a variety of other fruits and vegetables are grown. Sweet Vidalia onions, watermelons, soybeans, sweet potatoes, and sugarcane are harvested in the south's farms and **orchards**. Like the peach, the Vidalia onion is important to Georgia's identity and the state's farming history. It gets its name from a Vidalia farmers' market where the sweet onion first became popular.

Farther south, past the farms, the soil becomes sandier. On the southeastern edge of the region, just south of Waycross, is the Okefenokee Swamp. This nearly 700-square-mile (1,800 square kilometer) wilderness of black water, once the hunting grounds of the Creek tribes, is now the site of a national wildlife refuge. Oka means "water," and fenoke means "shaking" in the Hitchiti language. Over time, Okefenokee has come to mean the "land of the trembling earth."

The area was once a large sandbar—a ridge of sand created by water currents—under the

Vidalia Onions

The Vidalia onion is so sweet that some people eat it raw, like an apple. Named for the city of Vidalia, the onions are so unusually sweet because they are grown in soil with a very low sulfur content. By state law, an onion can only be called a Vidalia if it is grown in certain Georgia counties.

The Okefenokee Swamp, on the Georgia-Florida border, was designated a National Wildlife Refuge in 1937.

Atlantic Ocean. As the ocean retreated, some water remained trapped in a pool. The pool filled with rainwater and runoff water and became a freshwater lake. The fresh water became full of vegetation, such as dead leaves. As the vegetation decayed, the swamp was born. Although the swamp looks dark and dirty, the color comes from the tannins in the decaying leaves. The dark water is water is safe for animals to drink.

Along the Atlantic Coast, natural forces formed barrier islands and **marshes**. Barrier islands are long and narrow islands that are formed by waves, currents, and winds near a seashore. These kinds of islands, common on the Atlantic Coast of North America, are rare throughout the rest of the world. Barrier island chains lie along only 2.2 percent of the world's coastlines.

Sixty million years ago, southern Georgia was under water. Today, miners often find fossilized bones of prehistoric whales, sharks, and other marine creatures. The towns of Savannah, Darien, and Brunswick are built on land that was a string of barrier islands during ancient times. The islands formed when the sea level was 15 feet to 25 feet (5 m to 8 m) higher than it is now. As the water receded, the coastline moved eastward.

Georgia's coast has changed dramatically over the ages. Around eighteen thousand years ago, during the last **Ice Age**, the sea level was 400 feet (120 m) lower, and the

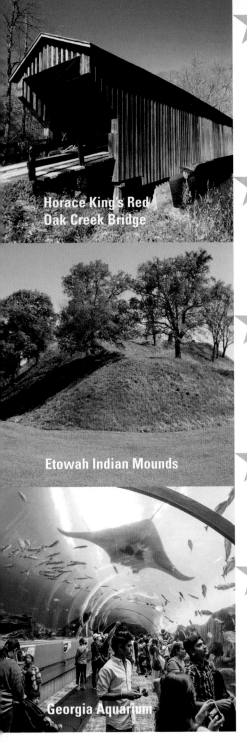

Horace King's Red Oak Creek Bridge

Etowah Indian Mounds

Georgia Aquarium

1. Black Heritage Trail

The walking trail winds through urban Columbus, passing thirty sites that honor African American history and **civil rights** achievements in the city. Featured are figures such as Blues legend Ma Rainey, and Horace King, a **slave** who became a master bridge builder.

2. Blue Ridge Mountains Art Center

The Art Center, in the historic Fannin County Courthouse in Blue Ridge, displays more than 2,500 pieces of art. Its goal is to provide a haven where artists can bring their work to the public. It is the largest gallery in North Georgia.

3. Etowah Indian Mounds

This 54-acre (21.9 ha) site near Cartersville features mounds and artifacts of the culture that lived in the area from 1000 to 1500 CE. There is a museum and a trail from which you can view the mounds built by Georgia's earliest inhabitants.

4. Georgia Aquarium

This huge aquarium in Atlanta has beluga whales, dolphins, sea otters, penguins, and exhibits that explore a variety of marine ecosystems. You can even swim with whale sharks.

5. Imagine It! The Children's Museum of Atlanta

Billed as "a smart place to play," the children's museum in Atlanta lets kids discover science and practice creative thinking in a fun environment. The museum is hands-on and interactive, so kids can experience the wonders of science and technology.

6. Museum of Design Atlanta

Known as MODA, the Museum of Design Atlanta is the only museum in the Southeast devoted to design, including the design of products, furniture, architecture, and fashion.

7. Okefenokee National Wildlife Refuge

This 402,000-acre (162,684 ha) wilderness in southeast Georgia and Florida is part of the Okefenokee Swamp. Visitors can hike, canoe, or drive through stunning wilderness areas and see 234 kinds of birds, fifty kinds of mammals, sixty-four kinds of reptiles, and much more.

8. Rock City

Signs on barns around the Southeast direct drivers to "See Rock City" on the Georgia-Tennessee border. Thousands come to see the mountaintop boulders that form city streets. They come for Ruby Falls, a waterfall inside a mountain, and for Lookout Mountain attractions.

9. Stone Mountain Park

Stone Mountain in Dekalb County features the largest bas-relief carving in the world. It depicts Stonewall Jackson, Robert E. Lee, and Jefferson Davis. There is a theme park with a sky ride, scenic railroad, historical exhibits, and more.

10. Tellus Science Museum

This museum in Cartersville includes exhibits on the history of transportation from cars to space exploration, a gem exhibit, and fossils of dinosaurs and other extinct animals. It also has a hands-on, interactive section for young scientists.

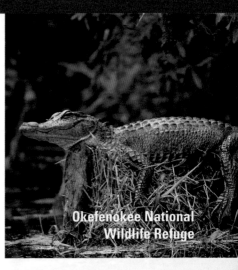

Okefenokee National Wildlife Refuge

Rock City

Tellus Science Museum

coastline was 95 miles (153 km) east of where it is now. Along the Atlantic Coast, nature's handiwork is still not done. The winds and tides are making constant revisions.

The Waterways

Georgia's Atlantic Coast is more than 100 miles (160 km) long. When sea levels rose, sand dunes along the shoreline became islands and the protected areas between the islands and the mainland became lagoons. These lagoons eventually developed into the salt marshes of Georgia. Crabs, oysters, mussels, and shrimp populate these marshes, but few plants except for tall grass survive.

The marshes form a long waterway known as the Inland Passage. This water highway is protected from the wilder weather out on the Atlantic, making it possible for small boats to move along the coast even during storms at sea. Only a couple of areas along the Inland Passage are bad for boat travel. These shallow spots are known as the narrows. At times, it is necessary to dredge them. Dredging is the process of gathering materials from the bottom of the water and moving them elsewhere, so that the water becomes deeper and ships can safely pass without becoming grounded.

The major rivers in Georgia are the Chattahoochee, the Savannah, and the Suwannee. The first two start in northeastern Georgia. The Chattahoochee joins other rivers in the south, and its waters eventually flow into the Gulf of Mexico. The Savannah

The Inland Passage provides a waterway for boats as well as canoes.

flows into the Atlantic. The Suwannee begins in the southeast. It flows through the Okefenokee Swamp and northern Florida to the Gulf of Mexico. There are many other smaller rivers throughout the state.

Along the southern edge of the Piedmont Plateau is a natural boundary called the fall line. Waterfalls occur along the fall line, as river waters spill over the end of the higher plateau onto lower land. In Georgia, where early trade relied on using the rivers to transport goods and people, cities emerged at the fall line, where ships could go no farther inland. Augusta was built at the fall line of the Savannah River. Columbus is found on the Chattahoochee fall line.

Waterfalls grace more than thirty spots in the state. The captivating waterfalls in northwestern Georgia include the double falls in Cloudland Canyon State Park. Amicalola Falls near Dawsonville are the state's tallest falls at 729 feet (222 m).

The state has both natural and human-made lakes. Human-made lakes are created by engineers to store water, help control floods, generate electricity, and offer recreation. The Great Lakes of Georgia are nine such lakes. Many of the larger human-made lakes are in the northern part of the state, where the land is mountainous.

Climate

Georgia spans so much land that the daily weather varies depending on the region. The weather is affected by altitude, or how high an area sits above sea level. It is also dependent on how close an area is to the ocean. However, for the most part, the state has mild winters and hot summers.

Georgians experience a range of seasonal changes no matter where they live—though some of these changes are more dramatic than others. The trees of northwestern Georgia showcase colorful leaves in autumn. It is usually milder in the Piedmont than in the northern mountains. In the Piedmont, snow is rare in the winter, and the summers are very hot and humid, with frequent thunderstorms.

In the Okefenokee Swamp, the weather is mild in the spring and fall, but hot and humid in the summer. Winter temperatures vary between cool and hot in the daytime, occasionally going down to freezing at night.

The climate along the Atlantic is generally mild, with hot summers and cool winters. Precipitation, which is the amount of water that falls as rain or snow, is high. During summer, however, a high-pressure system called the Bermuda High settles in the southeast, and its winds affect the weather. The Bermuda High produces occasional droughts, or long periods without rain.

Nature's extremes are also on display where the North American coastline tucks inward, between Cape Hatteras in North Carolina and Cape Canaveral in Florida. This area, where the tides are particularly strong, is called the Georgia Bight. In some years, one or more **hurricanes** hit the coast. With winds up to 200 miles per hour (320 kilometers per hour), these storms can be devastating. The Georgia coast has a 5 percent risk of hurricanes each year. Major tropical storms can also come from the Gulf of Mexico, crossing the Florida panhandle and entering Georgia. The costliest storm to hit Georgia, Tropical Storm Alberto, arrived that way. It stalled over western Georgia in July 1994 and caused severe flooding, resulting in thirty deaths and $750 million in damage. August, September, and October are the most common months for the storms.

Wildlife

Georgia has hundreds of thousands of plant and animal species. Because the state is made up of such diverse regions, many types of trees grow well in Georgia. Birch, cedar, beech, and hickory trees are found in the state, as well as palmetto, oak, maple, and poplar varieties. The trees and other plants provide shelter and food for a wide range of Georgia's wildlife.

Bears, beavers, snakes, deer, foxes, and raccoons make their homes in forests, fields, and wetlands. Amphibians such as salamanders, frogs, and toads live in watery areas.

Whooping cranes find food in Georgia's waters.

Alligators swim in the shallow waters of the Okefenokee Swamp. Lake Seminole is a 12,000-acre (4,900-hectare) lake filled with bass. Largemouth, scrappy hybrid, striped, and white bass swim with catfish, crappie, and bream.

In some parts of Georgia, as is true of many areas in the Southeast, wild boars run free. Birdwatchers spot cardinals, robins, blue jays, catbirds, larks, and wrens in Georgia skies. On the ground, feathered species such as herons, egrets, and cranes search for food in the water.

In the Okefenokee Swamp, cypress trees draped with Spanish moss tower over the water lilies floating on the water. The fly-eating pitcher plant grows below the trees, as hummingbirds dart in search of nectar, and whooping cranes fly above.

Endangered Wildlife

One challenge facing Georgians is the introduction of **exotic**, or non-native, species to their natural areas. When non-native plants such as kudzu, wisteria, English ivy, and bamboo take over, they destroy native plants. Fast-growing kudzu from China and Japan, for example, is disrupting the growth of native plants throughout the Southeast. Kudzu can grow over an entire tree so quickly that the shade it produces soon kills the tree.

The same is true for invasive animals. European starlings were introduced in New York in 1890, and they have since spread to Georgia. Starlings and house sparrows, which were brought from Britain in the 1850s to help rid shade trees of inchworms, now vie with native species for food and space. House sparrows compete with bluebirds for nesting cavities, sometimes even killing bluebirds just to steal their nests. Fire ants were introduced in the South in the 1930s after cargo ships unintentionally transported them from Brazil. Now, they damage crops and electrical equipment throughout the state.

However, the greatest problem facing Georgia wildlife today is loss of habitat, as the population increases and more land becomes developed for homes and businesses. Shrinking habitats cause a decrease in species numbers and a loss in species variety. Clearing trees destroys animal homes and exposes the ground to more sunlight and drier conditions. This exposure can kill other plants and animals. Removing the understory (the layer of plants that grows beneath the tallest trees) exposes small animals to birds and larger animals that will kill them for food. Destroying understory also affects the animals' nests, shelter, and sources of food.

Concerned scientists and residents have worked together to protect the state's wildlife. Laws have been passed to prevent the harming of certain animals, including the manatee and the leatherback sea turtle. Special portions of land and water have been set aside and protected so that the native species can thrive away from humans. Pollution is controlled by laws and regulations. Knowing that their land—and all the life growing upon it—is very valuable, Georgians do what they can to protect and treasure it.

Azalea

Bald Cyprus

Barking Tree Frog

1. Alligator Snapping Turtle

The huge alligator snapping turtle can weigh more than 220 pounds (99.8 kilograms). It lures fish by wiggling a pink worm-like structure in its open mouth. Alligator snapping turtles are now protected.

2. Azalea

In 1979, the azalea was chosen as Georgia's state wildflower. Many colors and varieties of azalea grow across the state. A hardy plant, the azalea has vibrantly colored blossoms that usually bloom between March and August.

3. Bald Cypress

The bald cypress tree grows in swamps and along rivers, lakes, and stream banks throughout the Coastal Plain along the Atlantic. Birds and squirrels eat cypress seeds, and eagles, ospreys, and herons often nest in the branches. Cypress roots make "knees" that keep the tree stable in marshy ground.

4. Barking Tree Frog

Barking tree frogs can grow to be about 3 inches (8 cm) in length. The barking tree frog is nocturnal, which means that it moves around and eats at night. The noise that it makes sounds like a barking dog.

5. Beaver

Beavers are large members of the rodent family that live on both land and water. They are known for building dams out of sticks and logs. Beavers were almost wiped out in Georgia by overhunting, but they have rebounded.

6. Bobcat

Bobcats are found in forested and agricultural areas throughout Georgia. Bobcats can weigh up to 40 pounds (18.1 kg). They are tan with dark spots and a light colored body, and have a short, bobbed tail.

7. Coyote

Coyotes aren't native to Georgia, but they have moved into both the wilderness and the cities where the now extinct red wolf used to live.

8. Eastern Indigo Snake

The eastern indigo snake is the longest North American snake. It can reach more than 8 feet (2.4 m). It often shares gopher tortoise burrows, even laying five to ten eggs in tortoise burrows every May or June. These iridescent blue-black snakes are threatened.

9. Fox Squirrel

The fox squirrel is the largest tree squirrel in North America. Its body, including the tail, can be up to 27 inches (.69 m) long. Some are a typical brown-gray, and others have dramatic dark brown, black, and white markings. They have a variety of calls.

10. Mountain Laurel

The mountain laurel is found on rocky slopes and stream banks in the Piedmont, the mountains, and the Atlantic Coastal Plain. This evergreen shrub provides shelter for birds and small animals, but is toxic to humans and animals such as deer.

Bobcat

Eastern Indigo Snake

Mountain Laurel

These Gullah folk singers are descended from African slaves who lived on Sapelo Island. Staying in isolated coastal areas helped them preserve their culture.

From the Beginning

Prehistoric hunters moved into Georgia about twelve thousand years ago. Little is known about them, but their descendants left evidence of their cultures in the form of pottery and flint tools and weapons. Later, a group now referred to as the Mound Builders prospered in the area. They are named for the large earthen mounds they constructed for ceremonial, burial, and living purposes.

The mound-building Mississippian culture flourished from about 850 CE until the arrival of European explorers. It is clear from their artifacts, such as pottery, that these people were skilled craftspeople with a complex system of trading. The most well-preserved Mississippian cultural site in the East is Georgia's Etowah Indian Mounds near Cartersville.

By the time the Spanish explorer Hernando de Soto arrived in 1540, the Mississippian culture was in decline, and the Etowah Mounds site had been abandoned. However, there was still a strong Native American presence in Georgia. A large portion of the Native American population was destroyed by de Soto's expedition and the Spanish settlers who followed. Spanish soldiers killed or kidnapped some of the Native Americans, forcing the survivors into slavery. Diseases wiped out many of the others.

The Rock Eagle Effigy Mound is one of many ancient Native American sites in Georgia.

Those who survived the arrival of the Spanish retreated to remote areas. They became known as the Cherokee and Creek nations. The Cherokee, whose territory reached into what is now the Carolinas and Virginia, lived in the mountains of today's northern Georgia. The Creek Nation, also called the Muscogee, later became known as the Creek **Confederacy**. They lived in the eastern part of present-day Georgia.

The Europeans

In 1562, France tried to establish a **colony** in Port Royal Sound, with the help of the local tribes. Their arrival alarmed the Spanish, and in 1565, Spanish troops attacked and killed the French settlers. Soon after, the Spanish built a fort on Saint Catherines Island. From there, Spanish priests set out to convert the indigenous people to Christianity. Their missions, or religious settlements, were the first European settlements on the Georgia mainland.

Native American populations in the area began to decline. There were also Native American and pirate attacks on some of the missions. By the end of the 1600s, all the missions had been abandoned and there were virtually no Spanish settlements north of Florida.

The British had already colonized the coast farther north. In 1732, King George II of Great Britain sent General James Oglethorpe to create a new colony near Spanish Florida, as a means of defense. The first boatload of British settlers, led by Oglethorpe, landed in 1733. They named the area Georgia after their king and called their settlement Savannah. The Spanish invaded Georgia and attacked the English in 1742. After losing the battle, the Spanish retreated to Saint Augustine, in Florida, and did not return.

With the British came enslaved African Americans. At first, Oglethorpe banned slavery in Savannah. But before long, British immigrants were renting slaves from South Carolina. Other British settlers in Virginia and the Carolinas used slave labor to grow valuable crops such as rice and indigo, a plant used to make blue dye. Georgia's ban was eventually abandoned. By 1760, thousands of slaves had been brought into Georgia to work in the fields. Their forced labor made it possible for Sea Island cotton to prosper along the coast. Rice plantations spread up the Savannah River and down the Atlantic Coastal Plain.

James Oglethorpe was the founder and first governor of Georgia.

The American Revolution

In the 1760s, Great Britain began to enforce new policies in the American colonies. It imposed new taxes and restrictions on colonial trade that many colonists resented. In addition, some of the British representatives sent to oversee the colonists were of questionable character and not always appointed on merit, which made matters worse.

However, Georgia was the youngest colony, and many of its citizens had been born in Britain. Their ties to their "homeland" were stronger than those of people in most other colonies. When the First Continental Congress was held in Philadelphia in 1774 to discuss how the colonies should respond to British policies, twelve of the thirteen colonies that would become the United States sent delegates. Georgia was the one colony

The Native People

People had lived in Georgia for thousands of years before European settlers reached the area. The best known are members of the Mississippian culture. They are known for building earthen mounds, which were used for both practical and ceremonial purposes. The Mississippian cultures had declined by about 1500 CE. When settlers arrived in Georgia, the tribes present included primarily the Cherokee, Creek, and Yamasee.

The Creek were descendants of the Mississippian tribes, while the Cherokee people moved in from the north when the Mississippian culture declined. Still, they had many things in common. Since they lived in similar environments, their diets were mostly the same. They hunted deer, and used leather for clothing. They also practiced agriculture, growing squash and corn. However, the Cherokee and the Creek didn't get along very well. In 1750, the tribes had a fierce battle. The Creek lost, and were driven south beyond the Chattahoochee River.

When Europeans arrived, they brought new diseases that killed many Native Americans. For example, it is estimated that before European contact there were thirty thousand to fifty thousand Cherokee. After the 1738 smallpox epidemic, their numbers dropped to seven thousand to ten thousand. Despite this, the Cherokee and Creek had relatively good relations with the settlers early on. In fact, they are considered among the

The Cherokee built homes of mud and clay spread over woven branches.

"Five Civilized Tribes" because they accepted many of the colonists' customs, and traded pelts with them. After the American Revolution, the state of Georgia stopped seeing the tribes as allies. Instead, it looked on them as obstacles to further settlement. The tribes were forced to give up their land. Later, on January 27, 1825, the Indian Removal Act decreed that they be forcibly relocated to Oklahoma. Many tribe members died on the difficult journey, which is known as "The Trail of Tears." Some Cherokee and Creek fled south instead, becoming the Seminole and Miccosukee tribes of Florida.

Today, there are three Native American tribes recognized by the State of Georgia. These are the Cherokee of Georgia Tribal Council, the Georgia Tribe of Eastern Cherokees, Inc., and the Lower Muskogee Creek Tribe East of the Mississippi, Inc.

Spotlight on The Muscogee Creek

Muscogee (muss-KOH-gee, with a hard "g" as in "gum") Creek is a tribe that originally lived in the southeast United States, particularly in Georgia, Florida, Alabama, and North Carolina. Many were forced to move to Oklahoma, while others traveled to South Florida to become the Seminoles.

Muscogee Creek Children: Babies were swaddled, or snugly wrapped in a blanket, and strapped to a cradleboard made of wood or woven reeds. They could then be easily carried on their mother's back. Children played with toys such as beaded dolls. Older children played a kind of stickball game similar to lacrosse.

Villages: The Muscogee Creek built houses around a central village square. Houses had thatched roofs, and walls made of river reeds and plaster. Each village also usually had a big building for ceremonies, and a sports field.

Clothing: Most clothing was made of soft deer hide, though some was made from woven fiber. Men wore leather leggings and a breechclout, or strip of material that passed between the thighs and was held at the waist with a belt. Women wore leather or fiber wraparound skirts. They wore cloaks in the winter. Later, they adapted European clothes to their own styles.

Hair and Decoration: Men often shaved their heads, either completely, or leaving hair in certain places. They sometimes wore headdresses made of porcupine fur. Women usually had long hair, and they often arranged it in a topknot. Men were sometimes tattooed, and wore body paint during ceremonies or when going into battle.

American artist A.I. Keller illustrated *The Siege of Savannah*, which ended in a defeat for the colonial troops in 1779.

that sent no delegates. The Second Continental Congress began soon after the start of the American Revolution in the spring of 1775. At first, only one delegate from one part of Georgia showed up. But by 1776, Georgia was one of the thirteen colonies that declared independence from Britain.

In the fighting that followed, the British captured the port of Savannah, and by 1779, most of Georgia was officially under British control. Yet intense fighting raged in the Georgia-Carolina backcountry. As much as half of the property in Georgia was destroyed by 1783, when the American Revolution ended and Britain recognized American independence. The area recovered quickly when the fighting was finally finished, however.

Georgia officially became a state on January 2, 1788, when it ratified the US Constitution. With a new wave of immigration from other states and from overseas, the population in 1790 was more than double what it had been at the beginning of the war.

Cotton Is King

Before the American Revolution, the British and the Native Americans in Georgia struggled for control of land. After American independence, Georgia farmers moved west into the tribal lands of the Cherokee and the Creek. In 1838, US general Winfield Scott and his troops rounded up the fourteen thousand Cherokee who were still in Georgia, along with those from the Carolinas. The soldiers forced the Native Americans to march to Indian Territory, in what is now Oklahoma. The march was called the Trail of Tears. It took the Cherokee more than five months to walk the more than 1,000 miles (1,600 km) in freezing winter weather. One-third of the prisoners died from the harsh conditions.

Cotton Gin

An invention by a Northerner helped spread slavery. Eli Whitney's cotton gin—which separated cotton fibers from the seeds—lowered the number of people needed to make cotton. Cotton production quadrupled, and more slaves were needed to plant and harvest the crop.

The land taken from the native population was given over to the pursuit of profits. In 1790, several years after the end of the American Revolution, farmers in Georgia grew only one thousand bales of cotton. By 1820, Georgia's plantations were harvesting ninety thousand bales of cotton each year. By 1860, before the start of the Civil War (1861–1865), the number of bales had surpassed 700,000.

The rapid growth of the cotton industry was largely due to slave labor. By 1860, Georgia had about 465,000 African-American slaves, working in the fields and their owners' homes. Though there were exceptions, many slaves suffered terrible punishment and endured harsh living conditions. The plantation workers lived with little or no medical care.

In 1829, because of fear of slave uprisings, the state legislature made it illegal for anyone to teach African Americans to read or write. By 1833, slaves could not own

The Cherokee were expelled from Georgia and forced west to Oklahoma along the Trail of Tears.

Make a Pine Needle Coaster or Basket

Pine trees are plentiful in Georgia. Tribes such as the Muscogee Creek would use long pine needles to weave baskets.

What You Need

A bag full of pine needles
6–15 inches (15–38 cm) long
A large pan
Two cups of boiling water
Thread or raffia

Scissors
A large needle (tapestry needles are perfect)
A straw
Tongs

What to Do

- Put pine needles in the pan. With an adult's help, pour boiling water over the needles and let them soak for fifteen minutes. Remove them with tongs.

- Separate the clusters into individual needles. Cut a piece of straw about 1 inch (2.5 cm) long. With the needles facing the same direction, slide them into the straw. Don't fill it all the way. Slide the straw to the point-end of the needles. Thread your needle and tie a knot in the end of the thread.

- Starting at the end where the needles used to be joined, wrap the thread tightly around the cluster. At this point, you want to completely cover the needles with the raffia or thread. When you have covered about 2 inches (5 cm), start to curl the needles like a snail shell. After that, keep coiling the needles and make the stitches farther apart. Connect each coil to the one next to it.

- To add more needles, slide them into the straw at the end of your cluster. Make sure they overlap a little.

- Continue spiraling and stitching until you have the size base you want. You can either leave it like this to make a coaster, or lay the next spiral on top and keep winding upward to make the sides of the basket. Near the top, add fewer needles. At the end, sew the last needles down securely.

property, testify against whites in court, travel without a special pass, bear weapons, or work in printing shops. Slaves were considered the property of their owners, who could break up slave families and sell family members separately.

The rich plantation owners exerted wide influence. According to the US Census of 1860, twenty-three planters owned more than two hundred slaves each. Less than one percent of the state's white population was in the planter class, defined as men owning more than twenty slaves. Most white Georgians were self-supporting small farmers.

The Civil War

Slavery, and the treatment of the slaves, became a wedge between the states of the North and the South. In the industrial economy of the North, poor immigrants provided affordable labor in the region's growing number of factories. By the mid-1800s, slavery had been outlawed in most Northern states. However, the South had fewer people and far less industry. The success of the Southern economy relied on growing cotton, as well as other crops such as rice and tobacco, on plantations, which depended on the labor of slaves.

Slaves made up 44 percent of the population of Georgia at the start of the Civil War.

In the US Congress, Representative Alexander H. Stephens of Georgia worked with Northern congressmen to create the Compromise of 1850. This set of laws kept the peace between the North and South for ten years. However, the issue of slavery had to be addressed as the United States expanded into the West. The federal government needed to determine whether slavery would be legal in western territories.

During the 1860 presidential election campaign, Abraham Lincoln opposed slavery in the West. When Lincoln was elected in November, Southern officials felt threatened. Southern states began to secede, or withdraw, from the Union (another term used for the United States at that time). South Carolina seceded in December. Georgia followed in January 1861.

In April 1861, war broke out between the North and South, and Georgia's young men crowded the recruiting offices to join the army of the new Confederate States of America. By 1862, Georgia troop totals reached seventy-five thousand. The state's factories and workshops in Macon, Columbus, Savannah, Dalton, Rome, Athens, and Augusta produced cannons, firearms, ammunition, clothing, and other gear for the soldiers.

Union troops under General William Tecumseh Sherman tear up railroad tracks in Georgia.

Georgia's ports and railroad lines became major Union targets. In the spring of 1862, the Union navy landed on Tybee Island at the mouth of the Savannah River. On the morning of April 10, Union cannons fired on the walls of Fort Pulaski. The Union navy closed the port of Savannah to ships carrying much-needed food and supplies to the South. The Union army concentrated on destroying the rails. By 1860, Georgia had about 1,200 miles (1,930 km) of railroad track—more than any other Southern state. The Union strategy was to close off supplies by destroying the transportation system.

Deadly Prison

Andersonville was a notorious prison for captured Union soldiers during the Civil War. Of the forty-five thousand men held there, thirteen thousand died of disease and malnutrition. Today, visitors can tour the site and also see the National Prisoner of War Museum, dedicated to American prisoners in every war.

In May 1864, Union General William Tecumseh Sherman marched into Georgia with nearly one hundred thousand soldiers. Their mission was to seize Atlanta and cripple the Confederate war effort. The troops of Confederate General Joseph E. Johnston were able to slow but not stop Sherman's advance. Outside Atlanta, Confederate General John Bell Hood, who replaced Johnston, managed to hold the city for forty days, but Union forces gained the upper hand. On September 2, Sherman's troops entered the city.

In mid-November, Sherman left Atlanta in flames and began his infamous March to the Sea. Sherman and his troops marched toward the Atlantic Coast, creating a trail of destruction approximately 50 miles (80 km) wide. Farms and plantations were burned, livestock was slaughtered, and private property was stolen. Railroad tracks, bridges, factories, and mills were destroyed. The Union soldiers reached Savannah on December 21. The port city fell quickly.

On April 9, 1865, Confederate General Robert E. Lee surrendered at Appomattox Court House, Virginia, in effect ending the Civil War. A month later, Union cavalry captured the Confederate president, Jefferson Davis, near Irwinville in southern Georgia.

End of the 1800s

After the Civil War, hunger and disease ravaged the region. Georgia's war survivors struggled to make a living. To keep the peace, the US government began a military occupation. Georgia was governed as part of a military district that also included Florida and Alabama.

During the period of rebuilding that followed, called **Reconstruction**, Georgia's former slaves—now freed—were given access to courts, the right to own property, and

Morehouse College has educated thousands of black males since it was founded in 1867.

Augusta

Athens

1. Atlanta: population 447,841

The state capital, Atlanta is the hub of what is known as the Atlanta Metro Area, a region that is home to more than 5.5 million people. It is a center of commerce, and home to the world's busiest airport.

2. Columbus: population 202,824

Located in Muscogee County, Columbus recently passed Augusta as the second-largest city in Georgia. It is located on the Chattahoochee River, and was named after the explorer Christopher Columbus. It has a vibrant mix of the modern and the historical.

3. Augusta-Richmond County: population 197,350

This consolidated city-county is located on the Savannah River. It is world renowned for playing host to the Masters golf tournament each April. The city was named after Princess Augusta of Saxe-Gotha, mother of Britain's King George III.

4. Savannah: population 142,772

Savannah is Georgia's oldest city. Nicknamed "The Hostess City of the South," this port city on the Savannah River lures many tourists with its historic sites, beautiful oak trees, and its vibrant cultural scene.

5. Athens-Clarke County: population 119,980

This consolidated city-county is home to the University of Georgia. Even though the city is fairly large, Clarke County is the smallest county in Georgia. Because of the university, this is a region of great creativity with a vibrant arts and cultural scene.

6. Sandy Springs: population 99,770

Located north of Atlanta in Fulton County, this city was named after the area's natural springs. The springs are located in what is now the business district. The city has a large art festival each spring, and a community festival every fall.

7. Roswell: population 94,034

Roswell, in northern Fulton County, was named after Roswell King, who thought the area would be perfect for a cotton mill. Today it is a peaceful city that was recently named one of the top three places to raise a family.

8. Macon: population 89,981

Located in Bibb County in central Georgia, Macon is known as "The Heart of Georgia." It is home to several colleges and universities, as well as historical and cultural sites.

9. Johns Creek: population 82,788

This suburb to the northeast of Atlanta is located in Fulton County. It grew from a trading post to a prosperous city. The discovery of gold in the region led to the first US gold rush. The city has many festivals and is a golfing destination.

10. Albany: population 77,434

Named for the capital of New York, Albany is known for its tree-lined streets. Every March the city hosts a Mardi Gras street festival that features music until midnight, a marathon, and a half-marathon.

Macon

Albany

Martha McChesney Berry, who never attended college, was given honorary degrees for her work in educating the rural poor in north Georgia.

the right to make contracts. Some moved into Georgia's cities, while some stayed on the plantations where they had worked as slaves.

Even with greater freedoms, Georgia's African-American citizens did not enjoy much progress in day-to-day living. They were not, for example, allowed to testify against white Americans. By the 1870s, US occupation troops were being withdrawn from the Southern states, and white Georgians gained control of the new state government. Georgia's legislators voted to make **segregation**—the separation of whites and blacks—a matter of law. African American and white Georgians lived separately and used separate public facilities.

Economics also held back African Americans. The sharecropping system of farming came into wide use during Reconstruction. In this system, poor families, black and white alike, farmed land owned by someone else, to whom they paid a large share of the harvest as rent. At the same time, the farmer had to buy seeds, farming supplies, tools, livestock, and groceries from the landowner. Under this system, it was difficult for a sharecropper to make a good living under the best conditions. A bad crop year meant financial disaster.

Two African-American colleges—Atlanta University and Morehouse College—opened soon after the war. However, there were few educational opportunities for younger African Americans. The public school system, established in 1871, had one system for white children and another for black children. The schools for blacks were generally of lower quality than the schools for whites.

Tenant farmers of any race in Georgia had trouble getting an education in the late 1800s and early 1900s. This group included anyone who rented land for growing crops. Agreements with their landowners ranged from sharecropping to fairer setups, but most land rentals guaranteed a hard life for farmers and their families. The tenants living in the poor northern counties had little or no access to schools.

To help educate the local impoverished children, Martha McChesney Berry, the daughter of landowners in Rome, opened her own schools in the hills and mountains. She began by offering a Bible school in an abandoned church. In 1902, Berry used her 83 acres (34 ha) of land in Floyd County to build a boys' school. In 1909, she opened a girls' school. By 1926, the school had grown into a junior college, and it became a four-year college, Berry College, in 1932.

Ups and Downs

Between the Civil War and World War II (1939–1945), regional and individual fortunes rose and fell. Between 1900 and 1916, the value of Georgia's cotton crop tripled. When the United States entered World War I (1914–1918) in 1917, Georgia's economy received a further boost. Savannah became a major shipbuilding center, and factories in many other cities produced large quantities of war material. The period of prosperity ended in 1920. The price of cotton dropped from 35 cents a pound (0.4 kg) in 1919 to 17 cents in 1920. Then, the fields were invaded by boll weevils, an insect pest of cotton plants. Hungry boll weevils moved into Georgia after eating through crops in Texas, Mississippi, and Alabama. The Southern states that were dependent on cotton were hit hard.

In 1929, while Georgians were still contending with the fall of cotton prices and

Hookworm

During Reconstruction, up to 40 percent of Georgians and other Southerners had hookworm. This parasite burrows through the soles of the feet and causes weakness and anemia. Use of outhouses was encouraged to keep the worms, transmitted through feces, from infecting soil where people walked barefoot. By 1914, hookworm had been greatly reduced.

the boll weevil invasion, the New York Stock Exchange crashed. Within two years, the entire country fell into a deep economic slump called the Great Depression. For the first time since the 1890s, the price of cotton fell to 5 cents per pound (0.4 kg). Many Georgians had to give up farming and leave their land. Some relocated to other states to find employment. Those who stayed struggled to make ends meet.

For many, the only available jobs were in the state's textile mills, which turned cotton into cloth. At the turn of the century, many northeastern textile manufacturers had moved their mills to the South, where workers earned less money and worked longer hours. Working conditions in the mills became so bad that mill workers agreed to a general strike across the Southern states. They walked out of their jobs in protest in early September 1934. By the end of the second week of the strike, about forty-four thousand people out

Textile workers march for better labor conditions in Macon on September 3, 1934.

In Their Own Words

"I can make this march, and I will make Georgia howl!"
—Telegram sent by Union General William Tecumseh Sherman to General Ulysses S. Grant before his March to the Sea through Georgia.

of a workforce of sixty thousand had walked out in Georgia. The Crown Cotton Mill in Dalton closed while textile workers joined craft workers in a parade of 1,500 marchers, extending over eight city blocks.

The governors of North Carolina and South Carolina called out the National Guard to stop the strikes and force workers back into their jobs. But the governor of Georgia, Eugene Talmadge, went one step further and declared a state of martial law. Military forces usually administer martial law in an emergency to maintain public order and safety. In Georgia, the National Guard arrested sixteen women and more than one hundred men near Newnan and imprisoned them at Fort McPherson near Atlanta. The strike ended poorly for the unions throughout the South.

Talmadge was a forceful man. When a public board refused to lower utility rates, he appointed a new board. During his time in office, he resisted racial integration and civil rights for African Americans. He opposed President Franklin Delano Roosevelt and his New Deal programs aimed at helping the poor and the jobless. Voted out of office in 1936, Talmadge was replaced by Eurith D. "Ed" Rivers.

With the US entry into World War II in 1941, Georgia's economy improved, along with that of the rest of the nation. Government orders for military supplies rushed into the state's mills, factories, and shipyards. Bell Aircraft built a big factory in Marietta.

The recovery came with a human cost, however. About 320,000 men and women from Georgia were in uniform during the four years the United States was in the war. Of that number, 6,754 lost their lives defending their country.

The 1900s End

After the war ended in 1945, the South's industrial base expanded rapidly. Ford and General Motors built automobile plants in Georgia. Bell Aircraft reopened as Lockheed-Georgia. In order to work in the new factories, many Georgians left their farms and moved to the state's cities or even to other states. The middle class of workers grew stronger as jobs became more plentiful.

In this era of social change, the civil rights movement gained momentum. African Americans and others spoke out in favor

In Their Own Words

"I have a dream that one day on the red hills of Georgia, the sons of former slaves and the sons of former slave owners will be able to sit down together at the table of brotherhood."
—Rev. Dr. Martin Luther King Jr. in 1963

of desegregation and equal opportunity. In the famous 1954 case *Brown v. Board of Education*, the US Supreme Court ruled that segregation in public schools was unconstitutional. The Court required that all states integrate their school systems "with all deliberate speed."

The leaders of the civil rights movement included the Rev. Dr. Martin Luther King Jr., a native of Georgia. In August 1963, civil rights groups held a march and rally in Washington, DC, where King gave his now-famous "I Have a Dream" speech, expressing his hopes that all Americans could enjoy equal rights and equal treatment. The following year, with the support of President Lyndon B. Johnson, Congress passed the first civil rights legislation since 1875.

Martin Luther King Jr., seated in the center, grew up in Atlanta.

By the late 1960s, Georgia had still not complied with the Supreme Court's 1954 ruling, and Georgia's schools became a flash point for the civil rights movement. King was serving as a pastor at the Ebenezer Baptist Church in Atlanta and as president of the Southern Christian Leadership Conference (SCLC), an organization working for equal rights. Through his sermons and speeches, he challenged the lack of progress. By leading marches and demonstrations, King used nonviolent protest to help make changes happen.

King was assassinated in Memphis, Tennessee, in 1968. Georgia's schools were not fully integrated until the early 1970s, but King's legacy lives on. The Martin Luther King Jr. Center for Nonviolent Social Change continues his work in Atlanta. In 2011, a national monument in King's honor was opened on the National Mall in Washington, DC.

In 1972, Andrew Young became the first African-American member of Congress from the Deep South since Reconstruction. In 1973, when Maynard Jackson was elected the first African-American mayor of Atlanta, he also became the first African-American mayor of a large Southern city.

In 1976, Jimmy Carter, from Plains, was elected the first US president from Georgia. A former naval officer, peanut farmer, and businessman, Carter went to the White House after serving as governor. After leaving the White House, Carter became one of the country's most active and involved former presidents. On December 10, 2002, Carter received the Nobel Peace Prize for decades of work for peace, democracy, and human rights.

Georgia Today

In recent decades, Georgia's history has been forged by businesses and those who run them. Coca-Cola, UPS, the Home Depot, and Georgia-Pacific are among the many big-name companies now based in the state. Since the late 1960s, Atlanta has been the financial and industrial capital of the South.

New South is a term used to emphasize the change from the slave-driven economy of Civil War times to today's economy, which is based on high-tech industry. The New South is a center for modern service industries, such as finance, and for technological advancements.

As of 2013, 447,841 people were living in the city of Atlanta. The number of people living in Atlanta's metropolitan area, including Sandy Springs and Marietta, is far greater, however. This area is home to 5,268,860 people—more than half the state's population. Atlanta is a major transportation center, the headquarters of the US Centers for Disease Control and Prevention, and a key communications center.

Atlanta Tornados

Atlanta was hit by a tornado outbreak in March 2008. In a twenty-four-hour period, forty-five tornadoes hit between Alabama and the Carolina coast, with much of that activity near the metro area. It caused three deaths, thirty injuries, and more than $250 million in damage.

Businessman Ted Turner built and sold a large media, sports, and business empire in the city. After founding the Turner Communications Group, Ted Turner purchased the Atlanta Braves baseball team. In 1980, he started the Cable News Network (CNN), a twenty-four-hour all-news cable channel.

Downtown Atlanta and its skyline have undergone dramatic changes since the 1970s. After the 1996 Summer Olympic Games were

Atlanta is the economic capital of the South.

held in Atlanta, the most visible reminder was the new Centennial Olympic Park. In 2007, the World of Coca-Cola opened. It welcomes more than one million visitors each year.

But Georgia, of course, is much bigger than Atlanta. The cities of Augusta, Columbus, and Savannah and the county of Athens-Clark each have more than 100,000 residents. Many of Georgia's other towns have kept their down-home nature while sharing in the years of statewide economic growth. The people of Georgia support a thriving arts scene, from the symphony, ballet, and theater of the cities to the community arts councils and music venues of the smaller towns.

1. 800-1500 CE

The mound builders of the Mississippian culture lived in Georgia. They are mostly wiped out by diseases brought by the earliest Spanish explorers.

2. February 12, 1733

The first English settlers arrive in what would become Savannah. These "worthy poor" all got land grants.

3. May 17, 1749

Georgia trustees petition parliament to overturn its ban on slavery. By 1775, there were eighteen thousand slaves in the colony (outnumbering English residents).

4. July 4, 1776

Georgia joins twelve other colonies in declaring independence from Great Britain. Later, in 1788, Georgia is the fourth state to ratify the US Constitution.

5. May 28, 1830

The Indian Removal Act is passed. Over the next few years, this act forced members of several tribes, including the Cherokee and Muscogee Creek of Georgia, to relocate against their will to Oklahoma reservations.

6. January 18, 1861

Georgia secedes from the Union and joins the Confederacy.

7. January 15, 1929

Civil rights leader Rev. Dr. Martin Luther King Jr. is born in Atlanta. He helped promote civil rights using nonviolent civil disobedience, received the Nobel Peace Prize in 1964, and was assassinated in 1968.

8. October 16, 1973

Atlanta becomes the first major southern city to elect an African-American mayor. Maynard Jackson, a democrat, served three terms.

9. July 19-August 4, 1996

Atlanta hosts the Summer Olympics. It cost $1.8 billion and had the slogan "Come Celebrate our Dream." The event was marred by a bombing that caused the deaths of two people, and wounded 111 others.

10. February 27, 2011

Atlanta becomes the first city to demolish all public housing projects, replacing them with affordable mixed-income housing.

The Peachtree Road Race draws
thousands of runners to the streets
of Atlanta in the summer.

The
People

From historic Savannah, Augusta, and Darien to the modern Atlanta metropolitan area, Georgia is a state of contrasts, especially between the old and the new. Some families can trace their ancestors back to the original colonists. Others have recently moved to Georgia but already call the Peach State home. In fact, many people fall into this second category. New residents with new dreams are constantly showing up in Georgia. It is now the ninth-most-populous state in the nation. Georgia has about 3 percent of the total United States population residing within its borders. The number of residents has just about doubled since 1970.

The First Residents

Georgia's first inhabitants were Native Americans. Though the government forced many tribes out of the state in the decades after the American Revolution, some have returned or stayed in remote areas. They tried to maintain their traditional ways of life. Today, Georgia's Native Americans represent less than one percent of the population. They include the Cherokee, the Creek—also known as the Muscogee—and the Hitchiti, Oconee, and Miccosukee.

Dance and drum performances are among the highlights of powwows in Georgia.

When Native Americans were being chased from the state, members of the Georgia Tribe of Eastern Cherokee, also called the Georgia Cherokees, remained in the northern counties. The site of the last Cherokee capital, New Echota, is located in northern Georgia. Today, Native Americans live in numerous towns and cities, attending schools, working in businesses, and playing a role in government. Some are trying to revive Native American communities by building new settlements. In 2011, a group of Creek asked the US government to recognize land on the Georgia coast as a reservation.

The Early Settlers

In the early 1700s, British settlers, some with African-American slaves, lived along the Savannah River. In 1752, there were about 3,500 European settlers and five hundred African Americans. When the British relaxed rules about land ownership, additional settlers and slaves arrived. In 1773, there were thirty-three thousand people, half of whom were African American.

Native American tribes controlled the lands east and west of the river until after the American Revolution. After the war, greater numbers of settlers spread throughout the region, taking advantage of free land. This settlement forced the Native American tribes farther west.

Many poor European immigrants or their descendants who traveled to Georgia struggled to survive in the backwoods. The more heavily forested, rocky, mountainous region of the north was much harder to farm than the coastal or southern regions. Many farmers in the northern regions had a hard time raising enough crops and livestock to feed their families. Of the 53,897 farms in Georgia in 1860, right before the start of the Civil War, only 902 were larger than 1,000 acres (400 ha).

The big planters, who owned huge plantations on which they grew cotton or tobacco, were the political leaders. They had the biggest role in what happened in Georgia during much of its history. Their advocacy of slavery and their insistence on laws that discriminated against African Americans later led to racial tension in Georgia.

Tenant Farmers

The Civil War brought great destruction to farms in Georgia. Farmers tried to restore their businesses and profits during the Reconstruction period but had limited success. After the slaves were freed, plantation owners were left without money or labor. At this time, many of these landowners entered agreements with tenant farmers. Sharecropping became a common practice. In sharecropping, a wealthy landowner allowed a poor person to use their land. The sharecropper had to buy seed and tend and harvest the crops. In return, they paid the landowner a share of the crops. Often that share was so large that the sharecropper couldn't feed his family, or went into debt. Sharecropping was practiced by both whites and blacks.

After the Civil War, many Georgians moved north, where the industrial revolution was in full swing. In the north, people could find factory work and homes in the growing cities. In Georgia, a small class of industrialists, whose wealth was not dependent on farming, began to arise. Still, it would be a long time before industry began to replace farming in Georgia. Many of Georgia's people, both black and white, struggled to make a living in the years that followed.

Despite the hardships, the population grew steadily. In 1860, there were just over a million Georgians. By 1900, the

Sharecroppers struggled to feed their families in Georgia.

★ 10 KEY PEOPLE ★

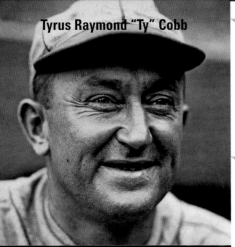

Tyrus Raymond "Ty" Cobb

Dakota Fanning

Juliette Gordon Low

1. Andre Benjamin [Andre 3000]

Known as Andre 3000, this singer, songwriter, actor, and instrumentalist was born in 1975 in Atlanta. He is known for being part of OutKast, the hip-hop duo that includes Savannah native Big Boi (Antwan Andre Patton).

2. Tyrus Raymond "Ty" Cobb

Born in Narrows in 1886, the fiery baseball outfielder for the Detroit Tigers was nicknamed the Georgia Peach. Ty Cobb made enemies with his hard play, but he recorded the highest career batting average at .366 and the second most hits in history with 4,189.

3. Dakota Fanning

Born in Conyers in 1994, this actress was the youngest person to be nominated for a Screen Actors Guild award at only eight years old. She has appeared in such films as *Charlotte's Web*, as the voice of *Coraline*, and Jane in the *Twilight Saga*.

4. Martin Luther King Jr.

Dr. King was born in Atlanta in 1929. He promoted nonviolent civil disobedience and is renowned for his "I Have a Dream" speech. The Nobel Peace Prize–winner was assassinated in 1968 in Memphis, Tennessee.

5. Juliette Gordon Low

Born in Savannah in 1860, Juliette Gordon Low founded the American Girl Scouts in her hometown in 1912. Today there are 3.2 million Girl Scouts in the United States, and more than ten million worldwide.

6. Margaret Mitchell

Born in Atlanta in 1900, Margaret Mitchell became a newspaper reporter for the *Atlanta Journal*. She gained international fame with the publication of her novel *Gone with the Wind* in 1936. The Civil War story has sold more copies than any other American novel.

7. Flannery O'Connor

This acclaimed author of two books and numerous short stories is one of the best-known Southern writers. Born in 1925 in Savannah, she writes in what is called the Southern Gothic style, making use of grotesque situations and disturbing characters.

8. Jackie Robinson

Born in 1919 to a sharecropping family in Cairo, Jackie Robinson broke baseball's color line when he played for the Brooklyn Dodgers in 1947. In 1962 he was inducted into the Baseball Hall of Fame.

9. Ryan Seacrest

Ryan Seacrest was born in 1974 in Dunwoody, an Atlanta suburb. After a career as a radio and television host, he got his big break in 2002 when he was hired to cohost *American Idol*. He also hosts the weekly radio show *American Top 40*.

10. Kanye West

West, born in 1977 in Atlanta, is a songwriter, rapper, music producer, fashion designer, and entrepreneur. He has sold more than twenty million albums and more than sixty-six million downloads.

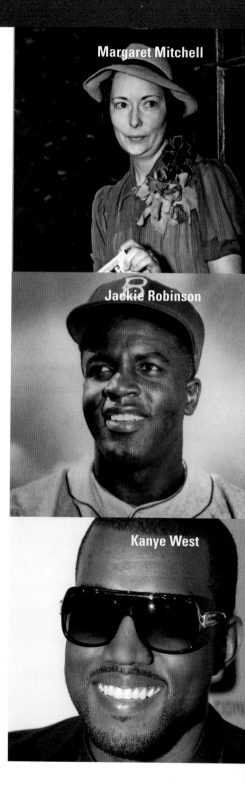

Margaret Mitchell

Jackie Robinson

Kanye West

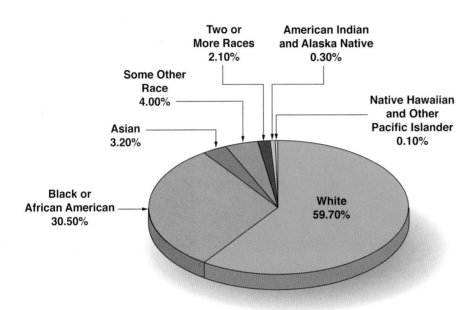

Total Population
9,687,653

Two or More Races 2.10%

American Indian and Alaska Native 0.30%

Some Other Race 4.00%

Asian 3.20%

Native Hawaiian and Other Pacific Islander 0.10%

Black or African American 30.50%

White 59.70%

Hispanic or Latino (of any race):

• 853,689 people (8.80%)

Note: The pie chart shows the racial breakdown of the state's population based on the categories used by the U.S. Bureau of the Census. The Census Bureau reports information for Hispanics or Latinos separately, since they may be of any race. Percentages in the pie chart may not add to 100 because of rounding.

Source: US Bureau of the Census, 2010 Census

number had doubled. At this time, most Georgians lived on farms or in small villages, and 60 percent worked in agriculture, most as tenant farmers.

Few industries came to Georgia from the northeast in the early 1900s. Some of the exceptions were cotton and lumber mills. Though these were part of the technological boom, they were the part that paid the least money. Wages were very low, and poor people didn't have the opportunity to improve themselves financially as they did in the North. The poor remained poor while the mill owners became even richer.

Through the late 1960s, many of Georgia's political leaders prevented the state from progressing socially and extending equal rights and equal opportunity to African American residents. Until January 1961, no African American attended school or college in Georgia with white students. Many Georgians worked long and hard for desegregation to finally happen in the 1960s.

African Americans

Historically, about 50 percent of Georgia's population had been black. For much of that time, the African Americans had been slaves, and afterward segregation and harsh laws made Georgia and much of the South an uncomfortable and even dangerous place for them to live. In what came to be known as the Great Migration, large numbers of

African Americans moved from the rural South to the industrialized North between 1910 and 1970. There, they could receive better education and have more opportunity for advancement.

After desegregation, many more African American people moved to the Southern states and especially to Atlanta, where the city's leaders worked hard to help the African-American community make economic progress. In 2006–2007, Georgia had the largest number of black people move to the state out of all the states in the US. Now it is third in the nation in the percent of the population that is African American.

Many of the new African-American residents are the descendants—children, grandchildren, and great-grandchildren—of families that once lived in the South. As a result, the people of Georgia started a new era of progress and opportunity.

Diversity

In the twenty-first century, people of many racial, ethnic, and cultural backgrounds make up the population of Georgia.

The Hispanic population in Georgia is expected to continue its rapid rise.

The number of Hispanic Americans in Georgia doubled between 2000 and 2010, and Hispanics now make up more than 9 percent of the population. The growth of the Hispanic population has been especially dramatic in the Atlanta area. Some Hispanics are counted in other groups, too. A Hispanic person might also identify as white or black.

When the Civil War broke out, about half the population of Georgia was African American. In the 1900s, African Americans from the South went north in large numbers. The 2010 US Census found that African Americans make up almost one-third of the state's population. The city of Atlanta has become a destination for highly educated black Americans.

Georgia is also experiencing a growth in its other minority populations. For example, the 2010 Census found that Asian Americans make up about 3 percent of the population. That is one percentage point more than in the 2000 US Census. In fact, Georgia had the second fastest growing Asian or Asian-American

Slum Theme Park

Americus is home to one of the most unusual theme parks—Habitat for Humanity's Global Village and Discovery Center. Visitors can see how terrible conditions are in a third-world slum, and hopefully be inspired to contribute to the Habitat for Humanity mission of bringing safe, decent living space to people in the US and around the globe.

population of any state in the United States between 1990 and 2000. The overall Asian population of Georgia nearly doubled during that time.

Age, Gender, and Identity

As with every state, Georgia has a diverse mix of age groups. There are a lot of young people in Georgia. About 7.7 percent of the population is younger than five years old. The percentage of people under eighteen years old is 26.4. These figures show that there are many families living in Georgia. It is also good news for the Georgia economy, as there are many young people about to be old enough to fill the many jobs in Georgia's industries.

A further 9.6 percent of the Georgia population is age sixty-five or older. These seniors are still a vibrant part of the Georgia economy. Among those who have retired, many have come from other states to live out their golden years in Georgia. People who have lived in the North are often attracted to Georgia's mild climate that still has a noticeable change of seasons, with lovely springs and the brilliantly changing colors of autumn.

Females make up a little more than half of the population—50.6 percent—while males make up 49.4 percent. The capital city of Atlanta is especially diverse. About 38.5 percent of the population lives in a single-person household (that is, not with family or a partner). Atlanta is also home to a large number of members of the LGBT (Lesbian, Gay, Bisexual, and Transgendered) community. Among major cities in the United States, Atlanta ranks third in the number of people who identify as LGBT, after San Francisco, California, and Seattle, Washington.

Languages

Georgia, like the rest of America, is multicultural, attracting immigrants from around the world. The primary language spoken in people's homes is English, with 87.35 percent of Georgia residents over the age of five speaking English with their families. Spanish is the next most popular language, with 7.42 percent of people in Georgia speaking it as their primary language. Other languages spoken in Georgia include Korean, Vietnamese,

French, Chinese (including Mandarin), German, Hindi, the Niger-Congo languages of West Africa, Gujarati, Portuguese, and French Creole.

Religion

Georgia, like most other Southern states, is largely Protestant Christian. Among the Protestants, Southern Baptists are in the majority, followed by Methodists, Presbyterians, and Pentecostals. John and Charles Wesley, the English founders of the Methodist faith, traveled to Georgia with James Oglethorpe and worked there for several years. Twelve percent of the population is Catholic, and 3 percent identify as belonging to another religion. These include followers of Mormon, Jewish, Muslim, Buddhist, and Hindu faiths. Thirteen percent are non-religious. This group includes atheists, agnostics, and deists.

Education

New Georgia residents come from around the country and the world. They are drawn to the educational, business, and cultural opportunities that Georgia has to offer. Georgia is home to some of the nation's best colleges, including the Georgia Institute of Technology,

rgia students outperform national average.

generally known as Georgia Tech. In addition, Georgia has sixty-two public institutes of higher learning (colleges, universities and technical colleges) as well as more than forty-five private institutions of higher learning.

Every Georgia student who achieves at least a 3.0 grade point average and attends a Georgia public university or college is eligible for the HOPE Scholarship. This scholarship is funded by the Georgia State Lottery. The scholarship covers full or partial tuition and an amount of money for textbooks for 120 credit hours, the number of credits normally required to graduate. Students must maintain a 3.0 average to keep their scholarship. If they fall below this, they can win the scholarship back if they bring their grade back up to 3.0 within 30 credit hours.

The state educates more than 1.6 million students in kindergarten through grade twelve. There are more than 2,600 schools in approximately 180 districts. The state's fourth graders are outperforming the national average in reading, according to the National Assessment of Educational Progress for 2011.

International Cherry Blossom Festival

Martin Luther King March and Rally

1. Atlanta Hong Kong Dragon Boat Festival

Every September, more than fifty teams enthrall spectators in Gainesville with their dragon boats. There are races, cultural celebrations that include many Chinese arts and crafts, and displays by the most talented entertainers.

2. Atlanta Pride

The largest pride festival in the Southeast takes place each October in Piedmont Park in midtown Atlanta. More than 300,000 people come to see the lavish parade and participate in the rally. This festival coincides with National Coming Out Day.

3. Georgia Peach Festival

Celebrate the Peach State every June in Peach County at the Georgia Peach Festival. Hosted by two cities, Byron and Fort Valley, this week-long festival has a parade, music, arts and crafts, peach-themed food and products, a Miss Georgia Peach contest, and fireworks.

4. International Cherry Blossom Festival

Every March, Macon becomes a floral dream as more than 300,000 cherry trees bloom. Over the ten days of their most spectacular foliage, Macon plays host to events that celebrate the trees.

5. Martin Luther King March and Rally

This celebration of civil rights hero Martin Luther King Jr.'s life takes place on the street where he was born, as well as elsewhere in Atlanta. The multi-day event held every January culminates in a march and rally to help keep his dream alive.

6. Mossy Creek Barnyard Festival

Visitors can have twice the fun at this festival, named one of the top twenty in the South. It is held in May and October in Perry and Warner Robins. People can enjoy musicians, crafts, hayrides, a petting zoo, and some of the South's best storytellers.

7. Ocmulgee Indian Celebration

The largest Native American gathering in the Southeast takes place on the third weekend of September at the Ocmulgee National Monument in Macon. Dancers, storytellers, crafters, and reenactors celebrate the culture of the tribes with connections to the area.

8. Oktoberfest

Every fall, the quiet north Georgia city of Helen becomes the ultimate party town with Oktoberfest. Visitors can celebrate with German music, crafts, and traditional food. The days vary, but events often run from September through November.

9. Savannah St. Patrick's Day Parade

More than half a million people take part in the festivities surrounding the Savannah St. Patrick's Day Parade. The parade is in the Historic Park District.

10. Yellow Daisy Festival

For four days in early September, the Yellow Daisy Festival draws more than 200,000 people to Stone Mountain Park. Hundreds of artists and crafters show off their creations, and the festival also features children's activities, live entertainment, and plenty of food.

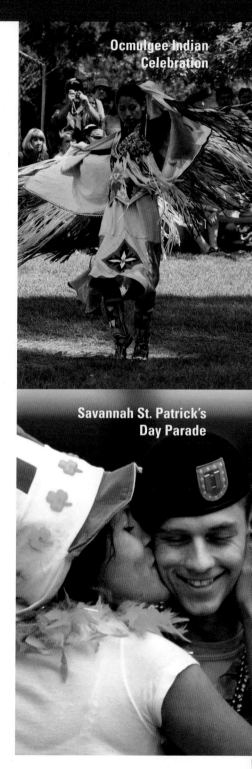

Ocmulgee Indian Celebration

Savannah St. Patrick's Day Parade

Georgia Governor Nathan Deal delivers the 2012 State of the State speech in the house chambers in the state capitol building.

How the Government Works

Georgia has 159 counties, more than any other state except Texas. Why does the Peach State have so many counties? Some say there was a rule in Georgia that every citizen should live within a half-day trip by horse or wagon from the seat, or center, of the county government.

Every part of Georgia, from the barrier islands to the mountains in the north, falls within a county. Local officials act as an arm of state government, performing many state-related functions, such as holding elections and issuing marriage licenses. Counties also provide a variety of local services to their citizens. However, the way that the counties operate is a local matter. Different types of government exist at the county level. County governments may be headed by a county manager, an administrator, or a commissioner.

The counties are made up of towns, cities, and other communities. Each of these communities has its own government as well. The local officials may be selectmen, mayors, or council members. Local governments handle issues that affect the town or city directly, such as parking regulations.

The capitol building in Atlanta was built in 1889.

Branches of Government

The state government, with its capital in Atlanta, has three branches. There is a legislature, which passes state laws. The executive branch, headed by the governor, carries out state laws. The judicial branch, which includes the courts, enforces state laws and can punish people who violate them. The highest court is the Supreme Court of Georgia. This court can also decide whether state laws agree with the state constitution, which describes the structure, the powers, and the limits on the power of state government.

Executive

The governor is the head of this branch. Voters elect him or her to a four-year term. The governor is limited to two consecutive terms, but a governor who has served two terms and is then out of office for at least four years may run again. The governor proposes to the legislature the state budget and new programs and laws, can veto (reject) legislation, and appoints many state government officials. The governor cannot, however, personally introduce a bill. The executive branch carries out laws and performs such government functions as providing education and maintaining highways. Other members of this branch include the lieutenant governor, attorney general, secretary of state, and superintendent of schools, as well as the commissioners of labor, insurance, and agriculture.

Legislative

The Georgia legislature, which is called the general assembly, is made up of two houses, or chambers. There is a house of representatives, which has 180 members, and a senate, with fifty-six members. All members of both houses are elected at the same time to two-year terms, and there is no limit on the number of terms a legislator may serve. The legislature has the responsibility of enacting new laws, changing existing laws, and repealing (removing) outdated laws or any other laws it concludes should no longer be in effect. The legislature also approves the annual state budget.

Judicial

Georgia's two major courts of appellate jurisdiction are the Georgia Court of Appeals and the Supreme Court of Georgia. An appellate court is a court that has the power to review and possibly change the judgment of another court. Georgia's Court of Appeals has twelve judges. It can hear any appeal from a trial court unless the state constitution directs otherwise. Judges who serve on this court are elected to six-year terms. The Supreme Court of Georgia has seven justices who make up the state's highest appellate body. They are elected to six-year terms as well. Any appeal that involves the interpretation of the US or Georgia constitutions must be heard by the Supreme Court. Elections for these judges are nonpartisan, which means that candidates do not run as representatives of a political party.

Georgia elects people to represent the state in both houses of the US Congress in Washington, DC. Like all states, Georgia sends two senators to the US Senate. The number of members a state sends to the US House of Representatives is based on population. Because the 2010 Census found that Georgia's population had grown significantly in the first decade of the twenty-first century, the state's number of representatives in the House increased from thirteen to fourteen as of 2013.

How a Bill Becomes a Law

The idea for a new law can come from any citizen or group, including students. The idea is shared with a member of the state house of representatives or the state senate. After the legislator considers the idea, shares it with other legislators, and discusses the legal meaning of the idea with a state attorney, he or she may choose to introduce it as a bill. A bill is a proposed law. When a bill is introduced, it is sent to a committee of legislators for further study and discussion. If the committee approves

Silly Law

Some people would think this is a matter for common sense, not an actual law. But apparently Dublin had such a problem that they needed a law. Part of the city code prohibits driving a car through a playground. Did someone really have to tell them that?

of the bill, it goes to all the members of the chamber in which it was introduced for their consideration. The merits of the bill are debated and amendments (changes) to the bill may be made. Then, the bill is voted on.

If most of the legislators do not agree with the bill and vote against it, the bill may "die," and that idea cannot become a law at that time. If a majority of legislators approve of the bill and vote in favor of it, the bill goes to the other

chamber of the legislature for its consideration. There, the bill goes through the same process as in the first chamber. If both chambers vote in favor of, or pass, the bill, it goes to the governor.

If the governor agrees with the bill, he or she can sign it into law. If the governor does not act at all, the bill becomes a law after six days if the general assembly is in session or forty days if it is not in session. The general assembly's regular session starts on the second Monday in January and lasts no more than forty legislative days. Those days don't

Senators discuss a bill, which must pass in both chambers before it can become a law.

have to be in a row. If the governor disagrees with the bill, he or she can veto, or reject, it. In many cases, a bill that is vetoed does not become law. However, the legislature can overrule the governor's veto if they have enough votes in support of the bill. To override the governor, both chambers must vote in favor of the bill by a two-thirds majority. If they do, then the bill becomes law despite the governor's objection.

Recently, the legislature has considered a variety of bills, from a ban on texting while driving to a bill that would require drug testing for individuals seeking public assistance. Some bills cover minor issues, such as how meetings are handled. Others address major issues, such as undocumented immigration.

Students presented a plan for cleaning the Chattahoochee River.

Taking the Lead

Some students in Georgia were able to get an important bill passed that allowed them to raise money to clean a local water source. Storm-water runoff from the school building, parking lot, and sports fields was draining straight into a creek that flows into the Chattahoochee River—the main source of drinking water for Atlanta. The students decided to make a wetland, building a ditch with water and plants usually found in natural wetlands, such as cattails, reeds, and rushes. Such a wetland naturally removes up to 80 percent of pollutants in wastewater passing through it.

The Georgia students got legislators to help them obtain a grant, or money, for the project. Ultimately, the state passed a law offering a reduction of property taxes to any citizen who built and used constructed wetlands on their property. Now, the water of Georgia will be cleaner and safer for everyone.

POLITICAL ★ FIGURES
FROM GEORGIA

★ Jimmy Carter: President of the United States, 1977-1981

President Carter grew up in rural Georgia and made a living as a peanut farmer. He served two terms as a state senator and one term as governor. In 1976, he was elected US president. After leaving office, he continued to be an advocate for human rights, peace, and fair elections. He was awarded the Nobel Peace Prize in 2002.

★ Nathan Deal: Governor of Georgia, 2011-

Nathan Deal began his political career as a Democrat. He was elected to the House of Representatives in 1992. In 1995, he became a Republican. As governor, he has made an effort to improve the criminal justice system, to reduce minority arrests, and help reform low-risk criminals. He was elected to a second term in November 2014.

★ Maynard Jackson: Atlanta Mayor, 1974-1982, 1990-1994

Democrat Maynard Jackson graduated from Morehouse College at only eighteen and went on to get his law degree. Later, he became the first African-American mayor of racially diverse Atlanta. He served three terms. While in office, he made great strides in improving race relations.

GEORGIA ★ ★ ★ ★ ★
YOU CAN MAKE A DIFFERENCE

Contacting Lawmakers

Kids might not be able to vote, but they can certainly share their opinions with local, state, and national leaders.

You can find contact information for your representatives and senate members at **www.legis. ga.gov/en-US/default.aspx**. From there, you can click on either "House of Representatives" or "Senate" to find out more information about either branch. At the top of either page, click on "Representatives" or "Senators" to get the contact information for individual members. Although phone numbers are listed, it is a better idea to write an email or a letter so you can fully explain your thoughts.

Keeping Guns Out of Schools

In the 2013–2014 session of the Georgia State Assembly, a bill was put forward about expanding where people could legally carry guns. This bill was known as HB 512.

This proposed bill addressed many factors that would allow more people to legally carry firearms into more places. One of the most controversial aspects of the bill was a measure to allow certain

Politicians heard the peoples' protests on HB 512.

people to carry concealed weapons on college campuses and on school grounds of elementary, middle, and high schools.

When the bill passed with strong support in the House, some people jumped into action. Spearheaded by Andy Pelosi of Gun Free Kids, a petition was started. Many Georgia residents banded together to fight the bill and signed the petition. They had to make sure the bill was stopped before it was passed by the Georgia Senate.

The Senate and Governor Nathan Deal must have gotten the message. The bill died in committee during the Senate's session. As of now, no one may carry any firearms on a school campus in Georgia.

Atlanta, the home of Cable News Network (CNN), has become a communications and technology center.

Making a Living

For many years the Georgia economy was based on cotton production. As the state's businesses branched out, Georgia became known for what are now considered its traditional industries—pulp and paper, food processing, and textiles and carpets. Food-processing plants employ more workers than any other type of manufacturing in Georgia. These plants handle many farm products as well as chickens and other birds raised in the state's large poultry industry. The state's older industries have been supplemented by other areas of business, including aerospace and automotive companies. The Peach State has also been riding the growth in bioscience and high-tech industries. Service businesses such as call centers and firms selling financial products round out the modern Georgia economy.

Agriculture

In earlier days, agriculture was an adequate description of the food-growing industries in Georgia. These days, the more accurate term is agribusiness. This change better reflects the research and technology that go into large-scale agriculture. This sector of the economy produces $65 billion annually for Georgia. In 2010, the number of farms

Georgia is the country's largest producer of peanuts.

in the state totaled 47,400. Georgia is generally the nation's top producer of peanuts, broiler chickens, pecans, and watermelons. Other top crops include cotton, peaches, eggs, tobacco, and tomatoes.

The boll weevil nearly destroyed the US cotton industry. These insects were wiped out from several states, including Georgia, in the early 1990s. Cotton is now produced on approximately 1.3 million acres (526,000 ha) in the state annually.

Some other insects have been helpful to the economy. The honeybee industry is very important to Georgia. Although this industry has been part of the state's agriculture for only the past century, Georgia is among the leaders in the country's bee production. Honeybee pollination is vital to many of the state's crops, including watermelons, cantaloupes, squash, and tree fruits.

Some of the biggest challenges facing Georgia's farmers involve national agricultural issues. The shift toward factory-like farming controlled by fewer and fewer companies is impacting small farms and rural communities. These shifts have a negative effect on the biodiversity, or variety, of plants and livestock. In addition, the chemicals used to fertilize crops, to kill insects that damage crops, and to control diseases among farm animals can pollute the environment and find their way into human diets. A growing group of farmers in Georgia is moving toward organic farming as a way of providing safe, healthful, and nutritious food choices. They are finding that organic farming can also improve farm family incomes and protect natural resources.

Poultry

Of all the states, Georgia ranks first in poultry production. Poultry producers turn out 24.6 million pounds (11.2 million kilograms) of chicken and fourteen million eggs each day, on average. The poultry industry's yearly contribution to the state's economy is now more than $13 billion. Of course, all those chickens produce billions of pounds of waste per year. Some of the manure washes into waterways that supply drinking water. The manure pollutes rivers and lakes with hormones and bacteria that can cause illness, and with phosphorus, which causes algae blooms. The algae blooms then kill fish by reducing oxygen levels in the water.

A program sponsored by the University of Georgia has been teaching farmers how to manage the chicken litter. Options include reusing and recycling it. "The whole purpose of the plan is to teach farmers how to apply chicken litter correctly to soil as a fertilizer and avoid … contamination in soil and groundwater," poultry scientist Dan Cunningham has said.

Paper and paperboard are big business in Georgia.

Products and Resources

Pulp and Paper

Georgia is home to more than twenty pulp and paper mills that produce more paper and paperboard than any state except Alabama. Georgia's mills send $10 billion of pulp and paperboard products around the world.

Peanuts

Africans introduced peanuts to North America. Today, Georgia produces about 45 percent of the total US peanut crop. More than half the state's peanuts are used to make peanut butter. The Georgia general assembly selected the peanut as the official state crop in 1995.

Aerospace

Agribusiness

1. Aerospace

The aerospace industry deals with the technology, science, and business of flying in the atmosphere or in space. Georgia has more than five hundred companies involved in the aerospace industry.

2. Agribusiness

Agribusiness covers a variety of related industries, including growing crops, raising livestock, and producing products such as wines and cheeses. The industry also includes research into better methods of production.

3. Arts and Entertainment

The creative industries such as art, music, and theater, employ more than 200,000 people in Georgia. The cultural offerings contribute to tourism. Georgia also offers tax incentives to encourage movie and TV companies to produce their work in the state.

4. Automotive

Georgia is home to Kia's first manufacturing facility in the United States. Many other components of the automotive industry, such as car parts, are manufactured in Georgia. Georgia's ports also send automotive parts overseas.

5. Energy

Georgia is a center of alternative energy technology. It is the leading source in the United States for sustainable biomass fuel. It is also becoming a leader in solar power, with the University Center of Excellence for Photovoltaic Research and Education at Georgia Tech.

GEORGIA ★ ★ ★ ★ ★

6. Information Technology

Information technology (IT) uses computers and telecommunications to manage and transmit data, which is a necessity in many other industries. Georgia is fifth in the nation for software, telecommunications, and Internet services. IT is one of the top expanding industries in Georgia.

7. Life Sciences

The life sciences industries help improve the quality of life through research and innovation in health and medicine, biotechnology, and pharmaceuticals. Scientists in labs throughout Georgia are doing everything from searching for cures for disease, to making medical technology.

8. Manufacturing

Manufacturing is a broad category of industry that involves producing merchandise. Goods are often made in complex factories that employ many workers.

9. Tourism

With so many cultural, artistic, and historic sites and events, Georgia is a premier tourist destination. Visitors can choose the big-city vibe of Atlanta, or the down-home rural regions. Tourism brings $53.6 billion to Georgia every year.

10. Transportation and Logistics

Georgia is a center of manufacturing, so it needs a big infrastructure to help it move those goods around the world. From highways to airports, railways, and seaports, Georgia has the means to move goods. It is also home to many warehouses and storage facilities.

Tourism

Transportation and Logistics

Recipe for Georgia Peach Splat Cake

This is a super-easy way to enjoy Georgia's sweet, juicy peaches even when they aren't in season.

What You Need

2 16-ounce (470 mL) cans of
peaches in light syrup
1 box of yellow cake mix
1 stick of butter
Brown sugar (about ¼ cup or 6 mL
or more if desired)
Cinnamon (about one teaspoon or more to taste)
Other spices as desired

What to Do

- Preheat the oven to 350 degrees Fahrenheit (177°C).
- Place half of the yellow cake batter in a 9 × 11 inch (23 × 28 cm) or 9 ×13 inch (23 × 33 cm) pan. Pour the peaches and their syrup over the batter. (That is where the splat comes in!)
- Sprinkle the remaining half of the yellow cake mix over the peaches.
- Cut the stick of butter into 16 or more small cubes. Sprinkle them evenly over the mixture in the pan. Then sprinkle the brown sugar, cinnamon, and any other spices on top. (Some good choices are nutmeg, mace, ginger, or a pumpkin spice mix.)
- Place the pan in the oven, and allow to bake for thirty-five minutes until bubbly.
- Allow to cool slightly before serving. This splat cake can be served warm or cold. It is delicious with whipped cream, or vanilla ice cream.

Peaches

A Peach County schoolteacher once asked her class to identify the four seasons of the year. The response that she received was fall, winter, spring—and peach season. Georgia is known as the Peach State because of its reputation for producing the highest-quality fruit. The peach became the official state fruit in 1995.

Shrimp

Available in supermarkets and at roadside fish markets along the Atlantic Coast, Georgia shrimp are appreciated by many seafood lovers. Georgia's rich marshlands are relatively unpolluted, and they produce an abundance of shrimp that are especially tender, sweet, and meaty. Many people consider these shrimp to be the best in the world.

Pecans

Long before Europeans arrived in Georgia, Native Americans were enjoying the pecans that grew wild in the area. Pecan production is centered in Albany-Dougherty County, in the area known as the Pecan Capital of the World. Georgia farmers produce about 85 million pounds (38 million kilograms) of pecans a year.

Manufacturing

Georgia produces aircraft parts, automobiles, and military aircraft and missiles. Manufacturers of aerospace equipment with a presence in Georgia include Boeing, Cessna, Gulfstream, and Lockheed Martin. The state exports more than $2 billion in autos and related parts. The state is also home to the country's largest manufacturer of school buses, the Blue Bird Corporation.

Some of the largest manufacturers in Georgia are Kia Motors, the automobile producer headquartered in Seoul, South Korea, and the aerospace and aircraft company Lockheed Martin. About 11 percent of the annual economy is related to manufacturing industries, including food processing. Tyson Foods is one of the largest employers in the state.

Kia Motors is part of Georgia's $2 billion automotive business.

International Paper is another one of the largest companies, as is Shaw Industries, which makes carpet, tile, and other flooring. Some of the newest manufacturers to open for business in Georgia include makers of recycled glass surfaces, specialty chemicals, and bed pillows. Manufacturers of solar and wind energy products, such as solar panels and wind turbine components, have also recently entered the state.

Armed Services

The American military is one of Georgia's largest employers. Fort Stewart, Robins Air Force Base, Fort McPherson, Hunter Army Air Field, Fort Gordon, Moody Air Force Base, Kings Bay Naval Submarine Base, the Naval Air Station at Atlanta, and Fort Benning employ thousands of people.

Not only humans work for the military. Georgia's Fort Benning is a training ground for military working dogs. War dogs are credited with saving the lives of tens of thousands of soldiers dating back to World War II. German shepherds and Labrador retrievers are the most popular dogs used in combat because of their excellent temperaments, intelligence, and senses of smell, sight, and hearing. The US Department of Homeland Security and various police forces also use many of Benning's canine "graduates."

Georgia Works

Ever since the port of Savannah was founded and Atlanta was settled around a railroad terminal, Georgia has been an important transportation center. Today, Hartsfield-Jackson Atlanta International Airport is one of the busiest, if not the busiest, passenger airports in the world. Delta Air Lines is one of Georgia's larger employers. Lockheed Martin Aeronautics in Marietta builds military aircraft and employs thousands of Georgians.

As in most states in modern America, the largest portion of the work force in Georgia is employed in service industries. Many Georgians work for wholesale businesses, which sell goods in large quantities to retailers, or in retail businesses, which sell products directly to consumers.

Many other Georgians are employed in service industries such as health care, education, law, and data processing. Large numbers also work in finance, insurance, and banking, as well as in real estate.

In Their Own Words

"We become not a melting pot but a beautiful mosaic. Different people, different beliefs, different yearnings, different hopes, different dreams."
—Former president and Georgia native Jimmy Carter

The Atlanta Braves are among the many entertainment options for Georgia's sports fans.

An enormous number of people travel to Georgia for business and leisure every year. Tourism is a major part of the service sector of the economy. Museum staff, tour guides, servers at restaurants, and hotel workers earn money through Georgia tourism.

With so much to offer, it is no wonder that the Peach State continues to attract visitors and new residents. There are many universities and colleges in the Georgia University System, including the University of Georgia in Athens and Georgia State in Atlanta. The Georgia Sports Hall of Fame, in Macon, is the largest sports hall in the nation. Fans root for Atlanta-based professional teams that include the Falcons in the National Football League, the Hawks in the National Basketball Association, and the Braves in Major League Baseball's National League. They also root passionately for the successful University of Georgia teams, which play in the highly competitive Southeastern Conference.

Atlanta is home to the Callanwolde Fine Arts Center, known for arts education, along with the High Museum of Art and numerous other museums. In the northern part of the state, the ArtWorks Artisan Centre showcases handicrafts. There is the Musical Theatre Festival on Jekyll Island in the east. The Columbus Symphony performs in the south. In each region, for every season, there is a wealth of culture and entertainment to enjoy in Georgia.

GEORGIA
STATE MAP

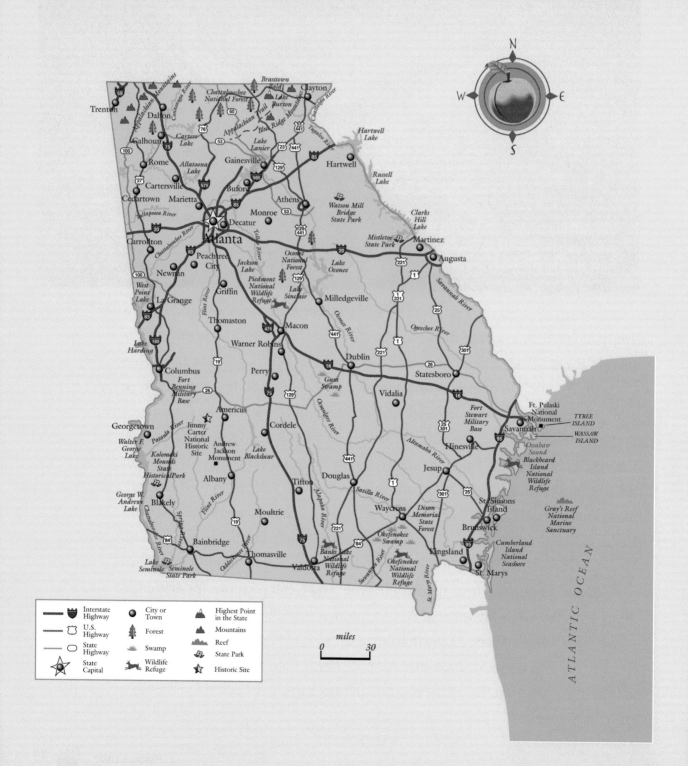

N
W E
S

Trenton
Appalachian Mountains
Commanga River
Brasstown Bald
Chattahoochee National Forest
Lake Burton
Clayton
Chattooga River
59
Dalton
76
60
Carters Lake
Blue Ridge Mountains
Appalachian Trail
Tugaloo River
Hartwell Lake
Calhoun
75
53
Lake Lanier
23 441
Hartwell
Russell Lake
Rome
100
Allatoona Lake
Gainesville
129
85
441
Cartersville
27
575
Buford
985
Watson Mill Bridge State Park
Clarks Hill Lake
Cedartown
Marietta
85
Athens
Monroe
53
129 441
Mistletoe State Park
Martinez
Decatur
Atlanta
Oconee National Forest
Lake Oconee
221
Augusta
Carrollton
20
Chattahoochee River
Tallapoosa River
Peachtree City
Jackson Lake
Tugalo River
129
1
Newnan
100
85
Griffin
Piedmont National Wildlife Refuge
Lake Sinclair
Milledgeville
221
25
West Point Lake
La Grange
Flint River
Thomaston
Oconee River
Savannah River
475
Macon
441
Ogeechee River
Lake Harding
185
Warner Robins
1
Columbus
Fort Benning Military Base
Perry
19
75 129
16
Dublin
221
301
Statesboro
26
Americus
Gum Swamp
Vidalia
16
Fort Stewart Military Base
Ft. Pulaski National Monument
Georgetown
Jimmy Carter National Historic Site
Cordele
25 301
Savannah
TYBEE ISLAND
Walter F. George Lake
Patula River
Andrew Jackson Monument
Lake Blackshear
Ocmulgee River
441
Hinesville
Ossabaw Sound
WASSAW ISLAND
Kolomoki Mounds State Historical Park
Altamaha River
Blackbeard Island National Wildlife Refuge
George W. Andrews Lake
Albany
Tifton
Douglas
1
Jesup
301
25
St. Simons Island
Blakely
Flint River
Satilla River
Gray's Reef National Marine Sanctuary
Spring Creek
Moultrie
Waycross
Dixon Memorial State Forest
Brunswick
Chattahoochee River
Bainbridge
19
221
Okefenokee Swamp
Cumberland Island National Seashore
Thomasville
75
84
Kingsland
95
Lake Seminole
Seminole State Park
Banks Lake National Wildlife Refuge
Valdosta
Okefenokee National Wildlife Refuge
St. Marys River
St. Marys
Ochlockonee River
Suwannee River

ATLANTIC OCEAN

Legend

	Interstate Highway
	U.S. Highway
	State Highway
	State Capital
	City or Town
	Forest
	Swamp
	Wildlife Refuge
	Highest Point in the State
	Mountains
	Reef
	State Park
	Historic Site

miles
0   30

GEORGIA
MAP SKILLS

1. What river flows along Georgia's western border?

2. What river, which shares the name of a coastal town, runs along Georgia's eastern border with South Carolina?

3. Which ocean does Georgia border?

4. Which national forest is along Georgia's northern border?

5. Which two wildlife refuges lie near Georgia's southern border?

6. Which city, Georgia's capital, is at the intersection of I-75, I-85, and I-20?

7. Which famous trail, named after the mountains it passes through, is in the north of Georgia?

8. Which river flows through the city of Dublin?

9. Which city is at the intersection of I-75 and I-16?

10. What marine sanctuary is located directly east of St. Simon's Island?

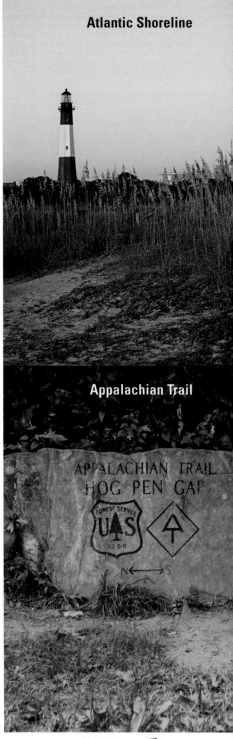

Atlantic Shoreline

Appalachian Trail

10. Gray's Reef National Marine Sanctuary
9. Macon
8. The Oconee River
7. The Appalachian Trail
6. Atlanta
5. The Okefenokee National Wildlife Refuge and the Bank's Lake National Wildlife Refuge.
4. The Chattahoochee National Forest
3. The Atlantic Ocean
2. The Savannah River
1. The Chattahoochee River

State Flag, Seal, and Song

There have been several versions of the Georgia state flag. The current version was adopted in 2003. It has three stripes, from top to bottom in the colors of red, white, and red. In the upper left corner it has thirteen white stars (symbolizing the original thirteen colonies) circling the state coat of arms (below), which is in gold.

The Great Seal of the State of Georgia was historically used on official state documents. On the front it has the Georgia coat of arms, an arch with three pillars, and the words of the state motto "Wisdom, Justice, Moderation." A soldier of the Revolutionary War stands with his sword raised to defend the constitution. Around the outside reads "State of Georgia 1776."

The back of the seal shows a large ship bearing the American flag arriving at Georgia's coast, as well as a smaller boat. There is also a flock of sheep, and a farmer ploughing a field. The inscription reads "Agriculture and Commerce 1776."

The state song, "Georgia on My Mind," was written by Stuart Gorrell and Hoagy Carmichael. Its most famous version was recorded by Ray Charles. It became the state song in 1979. To view the lyrics or hear a version of the song, visit this web site:

www.50states.com/songs/georgia.htm#.VEVtDT90xjo

Glossary

civil rights The rights belonging to a person by virtue of their citizenship, regardless of race, gender, or religion.

colony A territory that belongs to and is controlled by a country, but is generally far from it.

Confederate In reference to the US Civil War, of or relating to the eleven southern states that separated from the Union.

exotic From a foreign place; not belonging to that environment; an invasive animal or plant.

hurricane A tropical cyclone with sustained winds of at least 74 miles per hour (119 kmh), and as much as 200 or more mph (322 kmh).

Ice Age A period of colder than normal temperatures when glaciers expand.

native Of or belonging to a specific place.

orchard A place dedicated to growing fruit or nut trees.

marsh An area of wet, low-lying land characterized by few trees and an abundance of grasses and reeds.

plantation A large farm or estate in which mostly labor-intensive crops such as cotton or sugar cane are cultivated, generally by laborers (sometimes slaves) who live on site.

Reconstruction The period after the Civil War in which the South was reorganized and brought back into the Union.

segregation The act of setting a something apart from other things; in US history, it refers to the enforced separation of white and black people.

slave A person who is held in forced servitude and considered to be property.

More About Georgia

BOOKS

Bader, Bonnie. *Who Was Martin Luther King, Jr.?* New York: Grosset & Dunlap, 2008.

Cohen, David Elliott and Rick Smollan. *Georgia 24/7*. New York: DK Publishing, 2004.

Corey, Shana. *Here Come the Girl Scouts! The Amazing All-True Story of Juliette "Daisy" Gordon Low and her Great Adventure*. New York: Scholastic Press, 2012.

Miles, Jim. *Weird Georgia: Your Travel Guide to Georgia's Local Legends and Best Kept Secrets*. New York: Sterling, 2006.

WEBSITES

Georgia Department of Natural Resources: Wildlife Division
http://www.georgiawildlife.org/

The Official Georgia Tourism and Travel Site
http://www.exploregeorgia.org/

The State of Georgia Government
http://georgia.gov/

ABOUT THE AUTHORS

Karen Diane Haywood has edited many books for young people. She lives in North Carolina, where she watches the squirrels steal fruit from her apple trees.

Jessica Cohn has worked in educational publishing for more than a decade, writing and editing articles and books. She lives in New York State.

Laura L. Sullivan is the author of many fiction and nonfiction books for children, including *Under the Green Hill* and *Love by the Morning Star*.

Index

Index